A VISUAL HISTORY

Published by IWM, Lambeth Road, London SE1 6HZ
iwm.org.uk

© The Trustees of the Imperial War Museum, 2016.

ISBN 978-1-904897-52-1

A catalogue record for this book is
available from the British Library.
Colour reproduction by DL Imaging
Printed and bound by Printer Trento, Italy

All images © IWM unless otherwise stated.

Front cover: Q 729 (artificially coloured)
Back cover: Art.IWM ART 2957

THE SOMME

A VISUAL HISTORY

ANTHONY RICHARDS

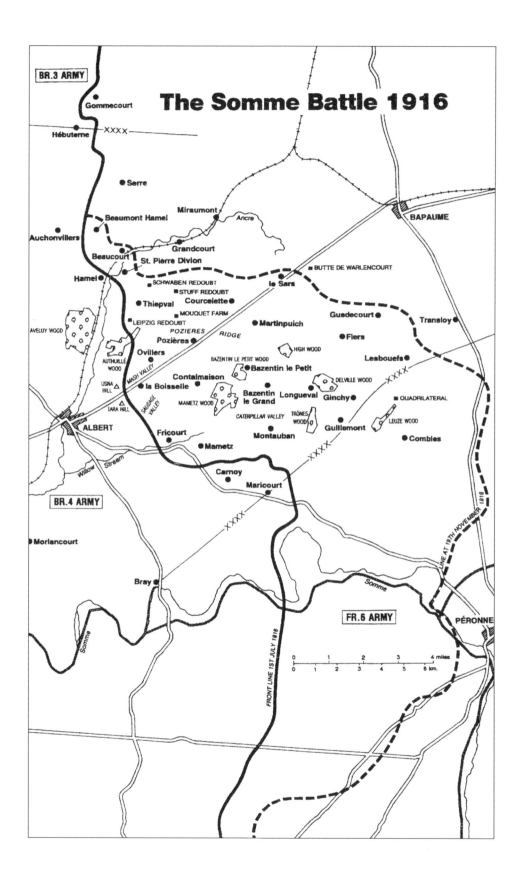

The Somme Battle 1916

BR.3 ARMY

Gommecourt

Hébuterne ××××

Serre

Miraumont

BAPAUME

Beaumont Hamel

Auchonvillers

Ancre

Beaucourt

Grandcourt

St. Pierre Divion

BUTTE DE WARLENCOURT

Hamel

SCHWABEN REDOUBT

STUFF REDOUBT

le Sars

Thiepval

Courcelette

MOUQUET FARM

LEIPZIG REDOUBT

Guedecourt

Transloy

AVELUY WOOD

POZIERES RIDGE

Martinpuich

Pozières

Flers

HIGH WOOD

AUTHUILLÉ WOOD

Ovillers

BAZENTIN LE PETIT WOOD

Lesbouefs

MASH VALLEY

Bazentin le Petit

DELVILLE WOOD

××××

USNA HILL

Contalmaison

la Boisselle

SAUSAGE VALLEY

Bazentin le Grand

Longueval

Ginchy

QUADRILATERAL

TARA HILL

MAMETZ WOOD

CATERPILLAR VALLEY

TRÔNES WOOD

LEUZE WOOD

ALBERT

Fricourt

Montauban

Guillemont

Combles

Mametz

Willow Stream

Carnoy

Maricourt

BR.4 ARMY

Morlancourt

Somme

Bray

LINE AT 19TH NOVEMBER 1916

PÉRONNE

FR.6 ARMY

FRONT LINE 1ST JULY 1916

Somme

0 1 2 3 4 miles
0 1 2 3 4 5 km.

CONTENTS

Flooded area in the Somme Valley, located near Corbie, 1916. This depicts the countryside well behind the British front line, giving some idea of what the French landscape was like before the major offensive launched in July 1916 further up-river towards Péronne. **Q 17486**

CHAPTER ONE

THE ROAD TO
THE SOMME

———————————

The land was not always associated with death. From the beginning of the First World War, the Picardy region of northern France had commonly been regarded as an unspoiled, quiet sector of the line in which a 'live and let live' mentality had been enjoyed between the opposing troops. But as the artillery bombardment began on 24 June 1916 – as a precursor to the Battle of the Somme – the valley and area around the town of Albert had become the centre of an immense build-up of the trappings of war. Over the previous months a massive body of soldiers had descended on the region, accompanied by the equipment, artillery and munitions to support a major army. When the battle proper opened on 1 July, it would have seemed that the land was the very epitome of a frenzied war zone, yet in the preceding years this had been far from the case. The landscape had even reminded some, such as the 17 year-old George Parker of the 1/6th Battalion London Regiment, of their English home:

> The country was still undamaged for miles at that time. It was agricultural land, with here and there a lovely little village in the traditional French style. A little church, a farm, a blacksmith's, an *estaminet* or inn, and sometimes a lovely chateau belonging to the owner of the surrounding property. It was winter when I first saw the Somme district. It was attractive then but in the summer, in peacetime, it must have been beautiful!

To understand how such a change was affected, and why the battle is still regarded as one of the key encounters of the First World War, we must first look back to how events had developed over the previous two years.

The assassination of Archduke Franz Ferdinand in Sarajevo in June 1914 had led to an international crisis in which the two large European power-blocs would come to blows: the German Empire and Austria-Hungary on one side, with Britain, France and Russia on the other. Over the previous half-century, the German Empire's economic growth and military successes and aspirations had created an atmosphere of growing rivalry, while the legacy of previous conflicts in the Balkans included a number of complex political and military alliances. In August 1914, the combined effect was a chain of declarations of war which many commentators considered an inevitable consequence of the long-running tension.

For many people in Britain, war was welcomed as an exciting opportunity to beat their German rivals. Yorkshireman Horace Calvert recalled how the announcement of war affected the people of Bradford:

Opposite This recruitment poster from 1915, illustrated by Frank Dadd, establishes a link between the older, distinguished war veteran and the younger new recruit equally keen to serve his country. The small British Expeditionary Force of August 1914 had to expand in size as the war developed and, by the time of the Somme campaign in July 1916, chiefly comprised young men with relatively little fighting experience. **IWM PST 11639**

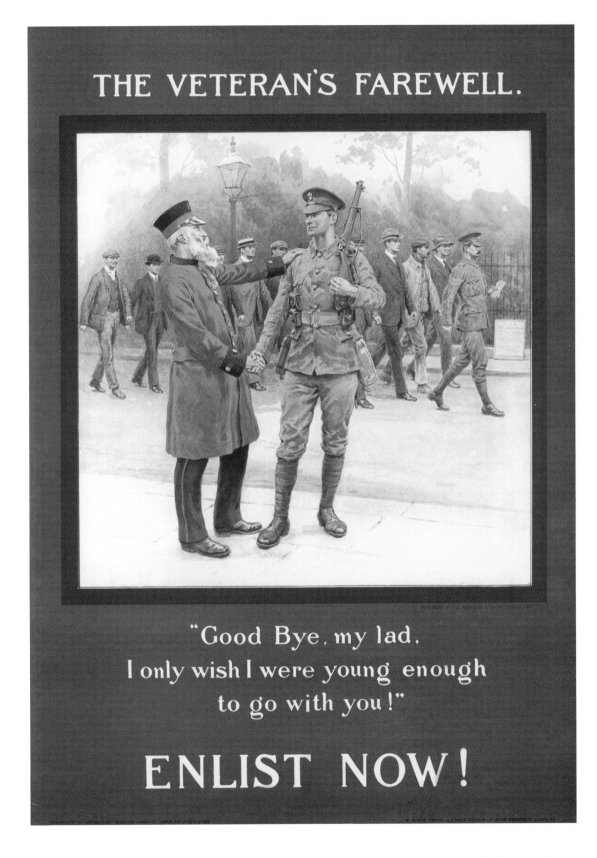

It was a lovely morning. I can remember it. I see it as plain as now. I was going to work for seven o'clock. As I got to the end of Richmond Road, there was a newsagent's shop and outside was a big placard, 'War Declared on Germany'. Mobilisation had taken place. In the evening I went to Bellevue Barracks. There were crowds round there, everybody was excited. Anytime they saw a soldier he was right at the top of the tree – cheering and all that. The people welcomed it: a challenge had been thrown down over Belgium and they were eager to take that challenge. Everybody was stood in groups talking, 'We've got to beat the Germans!' Quite a number were already setting off to enlist that day as it broke out. Very patriotic song singing – 'Rule Britannia', 'Land of Hope and Glory'. All the favourites. I stayed there till late at night – half past ten – I should have been back by nine!

On 4 August 1914 German troops had crossed into Belgium and attacked the city of Liège. Five days later a small British Expeditionary Force (BEF) of some 80,000 soldiers began to arrive in France and soon met the advancing German Army near the Belgian border. The subsequent Battle of Mons sent the BEF into retreat, and it was only at the Battles of the Marne and Aisne which followed that, with the added strength of the French Army, the German advance was halted and a series of manoeuvres began in which each side tried to outflank the other. This so-called 'Race for the Sea' resulted in a line of hastily dug trenches, reaching from the Channel coast down to the border with Switzerland. These trenches were adopted by both sides as a necessary but temporary measure to hold their current positions over the winter, after which they could marshal their strength for a renewed attack.

The ultimate aim was to resume mobile warfare in the spring, although in the event this would not happen for some years. The Germans made a strategic decision early on to dig in, with their trench lines protecting important captured ground which was to be fiercely defended. Concrete foundations, roofing and other practical innovations were introduced, with such well-constructed dugouts proving particularly important when fighting moved to the Somme in the summer of 1916. By the beginning of 1915, however, Captain Jack Cohen of the 1st Battalion East Lancashire Regiment was able to write home with a detailed description of both trench construction and what was by now the regular routine of trench warfare. It is this that would define the life of most soldiers for the next four years:

Soldiers of the 2nd Battalion Scots Guards dig trenches near Ghent, Belgium, October 1914. By the end of 1914 a trench line had been dug along the Western Front, running from the Belgian coast to the French border with Switzerland. This line would vary little over the next few years, with only a relatively small amount of ground taken or lost due to regular offensives. It would not be until the final year of the war that the deadlock was truly broken. Q 57167

Interior of a German dugout, complete with timber panelling and a brass bed, discovered at Fricourt in July 1916. British troops were astonished at the comfort of German living conditions. Since the adoption of trench warfare towards the end of 1914, the Germans had concentrated their resources on digging in and forming strong, semi-permanent defensive positions which could not be easily overrun. **Q 1384**

The chief business is revetting and draining, and improving parapets and traverses. Cover is got by building dugouts behind the trench. The bottom of the trench has planks running along it, otherwise progress is impossible. At intervals 'sump holes' the size of a coal scuttle are dug to receive the water which collects: thus baling is made easier. The parapet should be a couple of feet higher than a man standing in a trench. A plank is put at the bottom inside the parapet, sufficiently high for a man to fire standing. One man in four or six goes on sentry at a time. He looks over the parapet occasionally to see how things are progressing and is rarely hit in that way. When his first relief comes on, he does any baling that is necessary. Working parties are formed most of the night, and in the day where possible, to repair or rebuild damaged parts or make improvements. A party goes out after dark to fetch rations, and a small party before light for the rum. It is also necessary to send parties out for ammunition, etc. in the dark. We 'stand to' directly it begins to be light and at such times when heavy firing and cheering, etc., make it probable that an attack is in progress somewhere. We get our sleep not so much according to our inclination as when we are off work!

Once entrenched, it soon became evident to both sides that a quick end to the war was unlikely. Springtime 1915 marked a renewed attempt to break the deadlock with the Battle of Neuve Chapelle on 10 March. Responsibility for this chiefly British attack fell to General Sir Douglas Haig, commanding First Army. Haig and his subordinate in command of IV Corps, General Sir Henry Rawlinson, conceived a plan that relied on the power of a short 'whirlwind' artillery barrage, targeted to crush the German wire and other defences and thereby facilitate an assault by mobile infantry. The battle began well, with localised objectives successfully achieved including the capture of the village of Neuve Chapelle itself, but Haig's desire to continue the wider attack in the face of significant German reinforcements resulted only in the trench line being straightened rather than a more significant advance towards Aubers Ridge. The effectiveness of using massed bombardments was an important strategic lesson, which would be revisited by both men in the summer of 1916. Rawlinson would later write:

> What we want to do now is what I call 'bite and hold'. Bite off a piece of the enemy's line, like Neuve Chapelle, and hold it against counter-attack. The bite can be made without much loss, and, if we choose the right place and make every preparation to put it quickly in a state of defence, there ought to be no difficulty in holding it against the enemy's counter-attacks and inflicting on him at least twice the loss that we have suffered in making the bite.

However, to put this idea into practice on a large scale would require a significant concentrated artillery bombardment, and the British Army simply did not have this number of guns or shells in 1915. Rawlinson's 'bite and hold' tactic was too radical for immediate acceptance by the British and French High Commands, who favoured a more swift resolution to the conflict. They wanted to see a greater and immediate return on their huge investment in both men and guns.

The situation on the Western Front throughout the rest of 1915 was a continual disappointment to the Allies. The Second Battle of Ypres launched by the Germans on 22 April was marked by the first use of poisonous chlorine gas, leading to high casualties among the British and Canadian troops and their withdrawal to a new trench line at the edge of the Ypres Salient. As Private William Underwood of the 14th Battalion Canadian Expeditionary Force recalled, gas was an unpleasant new weapon, but one which the soldiers were determined to overcome:

General Sir Douglas Haig (1861–1928) commanded the British Expeditionary Force in France and Belgium from December 1915 to the end of the war. The Battle of the Somme would be the first real test of his military leadership, although many of the higher level strategy decisions were dictated by his French counterpart, General Joseph Joffre. **Q 23659**

We saw this green cloud come towards us, just slowly rolling along the ground, and behind it a grey mass of Germans in grey uniforms and some kind of respirator. They looked grotesque and we wondered, 'Just what is this? This isn't conventional'. We just felt terribly bitter: nobody's going to come through here and if we have to, we'll die here fighting. Our officer who was wounded told us to get out and meet them hand-to-hand for Canada. We felt pretty mad about the whole thing and no 'so and so' is going to come through here, even though we weren't equipped to hold them. Then one of our boys who was a chemist got a smell of this chlorine gas and advised us to urinate on our handkerchiefs or pieces of puttee or anything that saved our lungs from getting the gas. Well we knew that we just had to hold there – because up in the front line were our own boys who hadn't broken and run and there was this great gap with the Germans pouring through. We just couldn't leave – so we dug in with our trenching tools and hung on.

Lieutenant General Sir Henry Rawlinson (1864–1925) commanded the British Fourth Army throughout the Somme offensive. He is shown here outside his headquarters at Querrieu, a few miles north-east of Amiens on the road to Albert. The chateau became a British headquarters in early 1916 when the Fourth Army took over the majority of the front line, positioned between the British Third Army to the north and the French Sixth Army adjacent to the River Somme to the south.

Q 4032

At the Battle of Neuve Chapelle (10–14 March 1915), shells from a German barrage burst close behind the British front line trenches, preventing reinforcements being brought up. The success of the 'bite and hold' technique during the battle, advocated by Rawlinson in particular, would prove important to future campaigns such as the Somme during the summer and autumn months of 1916. **Q 49217**

By the time the German offensive fizzled out at the end of May, British casualties alone had reached 60,000 compared to the German 35,000 dead, wounded or missing.

May brought the next attempt by the Allies to launch an offensive, with an assault on Vimy Ridge led by the French Tenth Army, supported by an attack by the British at Aubers Ridge. Again, Haig's First Army opened its attack with a heavy 40-minute artillery bombardment, aided by mines which were detonated beneath the German positions. Cameron Ross was a Corporal serving with the 4th Battalion Seaforth Highlanders, and even before the main attack commenced, he became aware that the artillery had not done its job:

> The shrapnel shells were not doing the work they were supposed to. The wire was not being cut and, looking at it through the periscope, I remarked to the officer on duty that you might as well throw snowballs at the wire... after a terrible bombardment, one would think that everyone would be killed but when the whistle blew and the first wave of troops went over the top, they were all killed by machine guns. I heard the 1st Seaforth bagpipes play but, as they went down, one could hear only the drones. I ran towards the German trenches and got a bullet on one of my ammunition pouches which blew it up and I fell on my back. Thinking I had a bad wound, I put my hand down but, not feeling any blood, I got up and threw three bombs into the German trenches and then jumped into a shell hole half full of water. Seeing two wounded men near me, I crawled out and took them into the hole and afterwards got them back to their own lines. Waiting on the field all night I dragged several more to safety but since they were too heavy for me, I dragged them in on a waterproof sheet over the mud. During the entire time we were under fire.

The effect of the artillery barrage had been diluted by an inadequate number of guns and ammunition, coupled with the difficulty of covering three separate lines of German trenches. The subsequent infantry assault resulted in some 11,000 British casualties, with no material gain.

British involvement in the Allied autumn offensives was concentrated on the Battle of Loos. Once again, this attack was to support a larger French campaign, this time in the Champagne and Artois regions. Haig's First Army

An image synonymous with the Somme, and a sight shared by the many thousands of soldiers who trooped through the shattered town of Albert, this photograph of the Virgin statue hanging precariously from the Church of Notre Dame de Brebieres was taken in September 1916 when the battle was in full flow. A popular legend spread through the trenches that the war would come to an end once the statue, originally hit by a German shell, finally fell. Engineers made the statue secure, but it fell in 1918. **Q 855**

Inset Field Marshal Sir John French (1852–1925) joined the British Army in 1874, and served in the Sudan and South Africa during the Boer Wars. By 1912–13 he had been appointed as Chief of the Imperial General Staff, rising to the rank of Field Marshal in 1913. He was given command of the British Expeditionary Force on the outbreak of the First World War, but his failure to break the deadlock of the Western Front led to his replacement by Haig in December 1915. **Q 69149**

was to lead the attack, with Rawlinson's IV Corps and Lieutenant General Sir Hubert Gough's I Corps. Despite the British still being short of adequate guns and ammunition, the prolonged artillery bombardment which opened prior to the infantry assault on 25 September alerted the Germans and allowed them to bring up speedy reinforcements. Gas was used for the first time by the British, as recorded by Lieutenant John Pring, whose 187th Special Company of the Royal Engineers had responsibility for releasing the poisonous mixture:

> At 5.50 the [gas] jets began and on account of the dampness of the air, soon formed an obscure cloud in front of our line as far as one [could] see in either direction. The gas from here soon formed a dense cloud lying only a few feet above the ground and moving ... with the wind at about 2mph... At 6.30, the infantry advanced as per programme towards the German line which, in my part, was 400–500 yards away. These first troops encountered no resistance until they were out of my sight. However, they soon overtook the cloud on account of slowness of wind. Was informed afterwards that the first party had great opposition at the barbed wire, which had been very incompletely destroyed by our shrapnel. In my sector, the order was given to retire. All the foremost men were more or less gassed and a large procession of wounded returned and, later on, the advance was carried on by other troops and successive lines of German trenches were taken.

The village of Loos was captured but, as at Neuve Chapelle, relatively little ground was gained and any advantages to the new position were outweighed by the heavy casualties sustained. A similar story resulted from the French attack further south. Perhaps the most significant result of the offensive was a political one, as the continual military failures were deemed unacceptable to the public back home and changes at the top were called for. Despite the Allies having made a number of tactical advances – and learning from mistakes made along the way – this progress had been overshadowed by the German Army's considerable skill in defending their strong positions. The following year would see not only a concerted effort to break the deadlock of the Western Front, but a change in command at the highest level.

Interior of the National Shell Filling Factory at Chilwell, near Nottingham. One of the largest shell factories in the country, Chilwell was created as a direct result of the so-called Shell Crisis of 1915. The vast majority of workers were women, many of whom transferred from nearby textile factories. On 1 July 1918 a substantial part of the factory was destroyed by an accidental explosion, resulting in some 134 deaths.

Q 30018

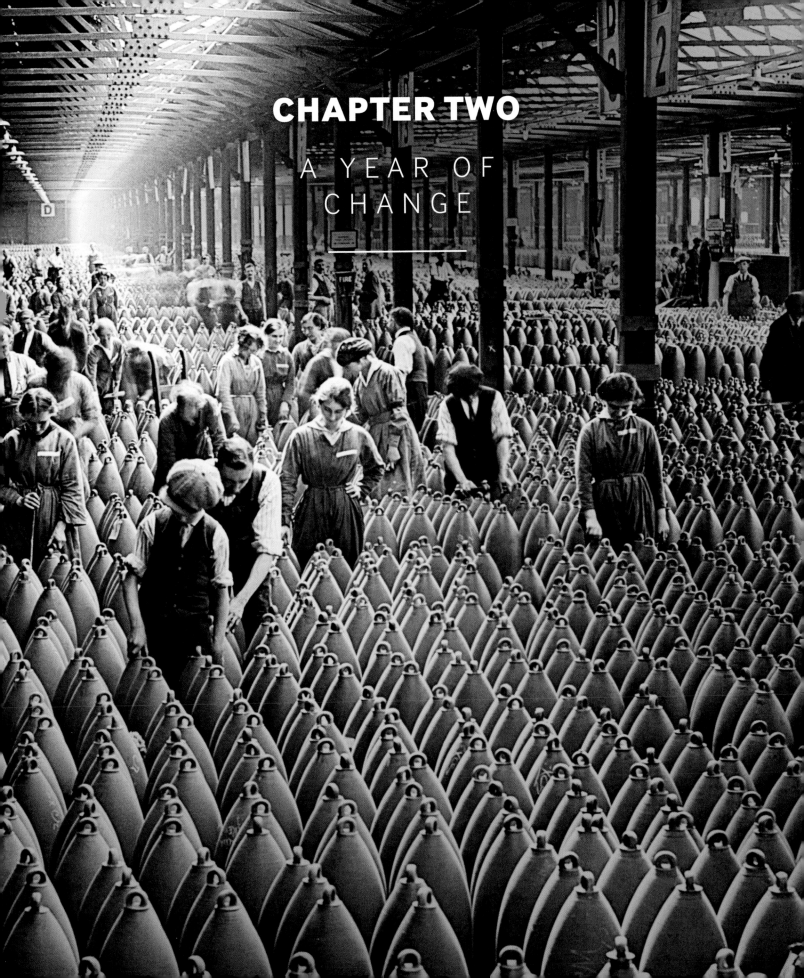

CHAPTER TWO

A YEAR OF CHANGE

The failure of the 1915 autumn offensive encouraged questions to be asked back home about the competency of the French and British military leadership. Criticism was directed towards Field Marshal Joffre for having failed to achieve success, despite so many French lives having been sacrificed, but his reputation as the victor of the Battle of the Marne helped to protect his position as French Commander-in-Chief. For his British counterpart Field Marshal Sir John French, however, it was a different story. As far as the British government were concerned, the failure of the Battle of Loos demanded a scapegoat and there was one obvious candidate. On 19 December 1915, French was replaced as Commander-in-Chief of the BEF by General Sir Douglas Haig. Another key appointment followed four days later, when General Sir William Robertson was chosen as the new Chief of the Imperial General Staff.

Above General Sir William Robertson (1860–1933) was Chief of the Imperial General Staff (CIGS) between 1915 and 1918. He shared with Haig the belief that the key to winning the war was to beat the German Empire on the Western Front in France and Belgium, as opposed to concentrating resources on fighting the so-called 'sideshow' campaigns elsewhere against Germany's allies. **Q 69626**

Opposite William Orpen, *Field-Marshal Sir Douglas Haig, KT, GCB, GCVO, KCIE, Commander-in-Chief, France, from December 15th 1915. Painted at General Headquarters, May 30th 1917*, 1917. **Art.IWM ART 324**

GHQ.
30th MAY 1917.

ORPEN

Opposite Flag carried behind Sir Douglas Haig on his various inspections of troops whilst he was Commander-in-Chief of the British Expeditionary Force between 1915 and 1919. **FLA 940**

Below In this photograph, Haig can be seen on horseback, accompanied by a standard bearer holding the flag, as he reviews Canadian troops following the Battle of Amiens in 1918. **CO 3014**

Robertson and Haig were united in a belief that all of the country's resources should be devoted to fighting the war on the Western Front. This change in thinking would have an enormous effect on the British attitude towards the war and the way in which the conflict was now to be fought. Beating Germany was perceived as the key to success since, without her support, the war efforts of her allies Austria-Hungary, Turkey and Bulgaria would all be likely to collapse. Destroying the main German Army should therefore be the chief aim, and this meant concentrating any fighting in France and Belgium, supported by the Russian presence on the Eastern Front.

Other commentators, led notably by First Lord of the Admiralty Winston Churchill and cabinet minister David Lloyd George, had felt that alternatives to the Western Front were preferable in order to avoid the high casualties which would inevitably result from a Continental war. The weakest points of the German Empire were believed to be its allies, and campaigns had therefore been launched against Turkey (at Gallipoli, in Palestine and Mesopotamia), Bulgaria (in Macedonia) and Austria-Hungary (in Italy). This view was perhaps encouraged by the British public's sentimental attachment to the importance of Empire and the country's traditional strength as an unrivalled sea power. Yet, as the war in these far-flung corners of the earth had so far shown, little success had resulted – with Gallipoli in particular being singled out as a disappointment which had led only to an embarrassing withdrawal in the face of strong Turkish opposition. Soldiers could be sent anywhere to fight, but trenches were not exclusive to France and Belgium, and stalemate was therefore the common result. The decision to concentrate resources on the Western Front was therefore a logical response to these unsuccessful 'sideshows' elsewhere.

The new year of 1916 also saw progress with regard to the problems of manpower and munitions production. Since the very beginning of the conflict, Field Marshal Lord Kitchener as the Secretary of State for War had been convinced that the conflict would be a long, drawn-out affair and by no means over by Christmas as many others believed. In 1914 he had begun to expand the British Expeditionary Force through a programme of recruiting many thousands of volunteer servicemen into a 'New Army', and the response of the British public to this call for help from a greatly respected military hero was unprecedented. The legal age for enlistment was 19, yet under-age volunteers were often accepted as long as they passed the basic fitness requirements and looked the part, as Harold Hayward could testify:

I went down to Colston Hall with the hope of enlisting in the newly formed battalion by the city, called 'Bristol's Own', official title, the 12th Battalion Gloucestershire Regiment. I went to the table and the recruiting sergeant was there. I knew that the age of enlistment was 19, so that it was no good me telling the truth – I would say I was 19 instead of 17 and a half. But I wasn't asked how old I was, I was asked 'When were you born?' I gave the answer I'd given throughout my life – 12th February 1897! The recruiting sergeant said, 'Well, I don't know whether we can take you at that age.' He must have seen my sad looks and he said, 'But if you go outside the Colston Hall, run round the building three times, you'll be three years older when you come back.' That was a good enough hint for me! When I came back he said, 'How old are you?' and I said '20!' So that got me into the battalion.

Until now the French Army had borne the brunt of the war on the Western Front, with the battles fought by the BEF being minor in comparison with the larger campaigns undertaken by the French. French casualties throughout 1914 and 1915 had been very high indeed, but crucially their sacrifice had allowed valuable time for the BEF to gather its resources and train its new recruits for active service. For the first time, fighting together as one British Army, would be men of the Regular Army, the 'weekend soldiers' of the Territorial Force and the new Kitchener's Army of volunteers – with the initial great test for these new legions being the 1916 campaign. The British fighting force would also be greatly expanded by colonial troops from its Empire, especially with the Gallipoli campaign having recently fizzled out. Soldiers from India, Australia, New Zealand, South Africa, Canada and other distant corners of the Empire were all keen to contribute to the war effort, and began to arrive in significant numbers on the Continent. As Haig took over in January 1916, the BEF was deploying some 38 infantry divisions on the Western Front, comprising almost a million men. Further batches of New Army and Territorial divisions would arrive by the summer, following completion of their training.

e the Guns!

ANKS!
ITIONS!

PRINTED BY CHORLEY & PICKERSGILL LTD, LEEDS AND LONDON

Another problem requiring resolution was the question of munitions production. The massive demand from the Western Front for shells had far outstripped production capabilities back home, and the battles of 1915 had suffered as a consequence, with many commentators blaming the shortage of supply. This 'Shell Crisis' led to the creation of a new coalition British government, under Herbert Asquith, as well as a new Ministry of Munitions, led by David Lloyd George. Women were recruited to work in factories in place of the men who were away fighting. Such munitions work was universally regarded as an essential way for civilians, and especially women, to contribute to their country's war effort. One 'munitionette', Gladys Quirk, put pen to paper in order to express her thoughts on her new employment:

My Brother is a Soldier
The only one I have got
If I had twenty more of him
I'd lend them all the lot

My Sister is a Civil Clerk
Helping her country too
Sorting out the letters for Soldiers
Also the lads in Navy blue

I'm just a Munition Worker
Toiling eight hours a day
Now we are being rationed out
We'll have to take what comes our way

I'm working my very hardest
And just going to test a shell
If I'd 'Kaiser Bill' here for a minute
I'd just fire him off to H___

Opposite Recruitment campaigns exploited the link between the field of battle and the home front by stressing the importance placed on civilians doing their bit for the war effort. In this example, the munitions worker shakes the hand of the soldier whom he is supplying with shells. **Art. IWM PST 5112**

British munitions factories finally stepped into gear, and by early 1916 were producing an unprecedented number of shells to feed the Army. This steady and systematic production at a higher rate now meant that, as planning for the summer offensive began, the desire at the front for concentrated 'whirlwind' artillery bombardments was finally beginning to be a realistic proposition.

Plans for the large Anglo–French summer offensive were made at Joffre's headquarters at Chantilly on 6 December 1915, for execution the following year. While the battle would be a collaborative attack, the French remained the dominant partner with more men in the field and arguably a greater stake in the war. To them it remained, after all, a question of liberating their own ground as well as addressing the wider issue of German aggression. Although remaining in overall command of the British Expeditionary Force, Haig had received direct orders from Kitchener to carry out Joffre's wishes on matters of strategy, and it was therefore the French Commander-in-Chief who would control the overall direction of the campaign. Indeed, the basic plans had already been put into place just prior to Haig taking over from Sir John French.

Picardy was the area chosen for the attack, in the sector where the French and British armies adjoined each other on either side of the River Somme. The French would launch an attack south of the river, while the British would attack to the north, both armies sharing a huge battlefront spanning some 60 miles. As Joffre himself announced:

> The French offensive would be greatly aided by a simultaneous offensive of the British forces between the Somme and Arras. Besides the interest which this last area presents on account of its close proximity to that where the effort of the French armies will be made, I think that it will be a considerable advantage to attack the enemy on a front where for long months the reciprocal activity of the troops opposed to each other has been less than elsewhere. The ground is, besides, in many places favourable to the development of a powerful offensive.

It was true that no major offensive had yet taken place in the Somme sector, and the surrounding ground had therefore escaped the whole-scale destruction that other areas of France and Belgium had suffered. However there was another, perhaps more important, reason why Joffre was keen on the idea of a joint Anglo–French offensive. By keeping the British on a tight leash, he could ensure that both armies would stay resolute to the main military agenda and prevent any postponements to the attack.

This message sent from Haig, praising the work of munitions workers at Gretna, was aimed at boosting morale among the workers and encouraging even greater production of shells for the front. HM Factory Gretna was the largest producer of cordite during the First World War.

At its peak, the factory produced some 800 tons per week, more than all the other munitions plants in Britain combined.

Art.IWM PST 13468

H.M. FACTORY, GRETNA

COPY OF LETTER

FROM

GENERAL SIR DOUGLAS HAIG

Commanding British Army in France.

General Headquarters,
British Army in the Field,
July 13th, 1916.

I feel sure that you would like to know how fully the troops in this country appreciate the strenuous and self-sacrificing efforts which are being made by their fellow-countrymen at home to furnish them with the quantity of ammunition necessary to bring this campaign to an early and successful conclusion.

At this moment we are engaged in the greatest battle the British Army has ever fought. Our daily progress has been continuous since the battle opened, but the successes of our gallant troops have only been made possible by the guns and ammunition turned out in the factories at home.

The munition workers at home very generously gave up their Whitsuntide holiday and were promised two days in August instead. I fully appreciate how tired they must be and how much they must be looking forward to that promised holiday. Yet, I feel confident that if they could but see their comrades fighting here, both night and day, with heroism and determination which is beyond all praise, they would not hesitate to surrender those two days' rest, and would devote them to maintaining and if possible increasing the supply of guns and shells, without which victory is impossible.

I ask you to put the facts before the workmen and I know they will consent.

Two days' cessation of work in the munition factories must have the most serious effect on our operations. It might even mean the addition of many months to the war. The pressure which we have now brought to bear on the enemy must not for a moment be relaxed. The troops are prepared and eager to maintain it, but the continuous supply of ammunition is a vital factor.

The Army in France looks to the munition workers to enable it to complete its task, and I feel sure that this appeal will not be in vain.

Let the whole British nation forgo any idea of a general holiday until our goal is reached. A speedy and decisive victory will then be ours!

D. HAIG.

Above General Erich von Falkenhayn (1861–1922), who was appointed as Chief of the General Staff of the German Army following the Battle of the Marne in September 1914. He believed that a strong German attack on the French fortress town of Verdun would act as the decisive action to remove the French Army from the war, but in the event the decision would lead to his own downfall. **Q 23726**

Below General Joseph Joffre (1852–1931) was Commander-in-Chief of the French Army from the outbreak of the First World War until December 1916. His reputation as a military leader was established when he successfully regrouped the retreating British and French in September 1914 at the Battle of the Marne. Joffre is shown here decorating and congratulating Private Jouy, a hero of Fort Vaux during the Battle of Verdun. **Q 70069**

Haig, as well as many of the other British commanders, actually favoured an offensive in Belgium so that the strategically important coastline could be liberated and controlled. Preservation of their alliance with the French was crucial, however, if any long-term success was to be achieved against Germany. But in the event, it would prove to be neither Joffre nor Haig who made the most important decision on the battle. The agenda was ultimately controlled by the Germans, when they launched a major attack on the French fortress city of Verdun on 21 February 1916.

The German Chief of the General Staff, Erich von Falkenhayn, believed that the war had to be won before the end of 1916 in order to prevent Germany collapsing under the pressure of fighting a war on two separate fronts. Just as Haig and Robertson had argued for a concentration of effort in France and Belgium, so Falkenhayn decided that the German Army needed to go on the offensive and seek a swift victory on the Western Front. While Austria-Hungary was busy fighting the Italians, and a swift defeat of the Russian Empire on the Eastern Front seemed unlikely, it made most sense to concentrate on the defeat of the French. Falkenhayn regarded the French Army as being in a weaker position than the British, due to their considerable exertions throughout 1914 and 1915 and the very high casualties they had already sustained. Closer to defeat, they would prove the better target.

In the Argonne region of France, the Germans began their artillery barrage of Verdun on 21 February. This was followed by a slow advance of infantry, which included the new German stormtrooper units – specialist assault troops who would rush to overwhelm the enemy's trench lines and eliminate their defenders. The French knuckled down for a long fight; the loss of Verdun would impact heavily on French national morale and was to be avoided at all costs. Retreat was forbidden, and attempts to counter the assault were put into operation. Efforts were made to avoid battle fatigue by constantly rotating troops at the front, while the French heavy artillery was repositioned so that they could fire into the exposed flank of the German advance. The battle was characterised by its harsh fighting conditions and the constant rain. While the front line was never static, it equally did not waver by much and, despite their capture of Fort Douaumont on 25 February, the Germans soon lost focus to the attack, being intent on pressing on with a war of attrition despite the logic of suspending operations or moving the main thrust of their assault to other areas. William Lafrichoud, a French Poilu based at Verdun with the 279th Infantry Regiment, described how his unit encountered one of the many regular enemy attacks on their trenches:

We had just finished our drink when there was an almighty explosion, shaking the ground under our feet. The Boche had tried to mine the fortifications, but the mine hadn't been effective and all those in the fort escaped safely. In an instant, Mezin let out a cry: 'The Boche'. The sergeant and I leapt for the gun, Mezin for his grenades. The Boche were coming towards us in the hollow in single file, 30 metres away. They were advancing slowly because of the heaps of broken branches from the trees. As quick as a flash, our three magazines were emptied at them. Just as quickly they flattened themselves to the ground and crawled on their hands. We didn't let up with our fire and Mezin threw his grenades. His aim was poor because he was nervous. Then he shouted, 'On the right, fire, fire'. At that moment there were branches in the way of my eyes, then I saw them crawling towards me 10 metres from the trench. The moment they stood up, I aimed at the one in the lead and fired. He fell dead. The others flattened themselves and retreated, crawling away. Right in front of me, one of them got upright behind a tree. I fired, but missed him. My round hit a stump close to his head and he flattened himself to the ground. At the machine gun at the corner of the trench they had seen the advance and were firing too, but the slope of the ground and all the tree trunks were such that it wasn't doing much good. Over to the right we could hear the clatter of our machine guns and the sound of grenades going off in front of the third and fourth platoons and the 42nd Chasseurs. They had bungled their attack, and withdrew leaping into a shell crater. Sibel came over to us. 'Look behind, the Boche are attacking with a flamethrower. It's the first time I've seen one, it's frightful.' Two flamethrowers were in action accompanied by grenadiers who were throwing their bombs. One of the companies had to evacuate their trench, but not for very long. One of the flamethrowers was hit and his appliance caught fire. The man was charred to a cinder. The other was so unbalanced on the slope that he fell in the trench. They said he was battered to death. The company regained the trench with grenades and it cost the aggressor dearly.

The sheer scale of the German attack at Verdun, and the need for the French to commit more soldiers to defend their position, meant that plans for the summer offensive needed to be rethought. The French Army could no longer make such a large contribution to the Somme, yet Joffre was keen for the British to continue the attack, playing a much greater role than had previously been envisaged. With the French in a desperate situation, and bound by the need to stay resolute to the Anglo–French alliance, Haig had little choice but to comply.

Two French soldiers, dead and half-buried in the soil, killed during the bitter fighting for Fort Vaux in the Battle of Verdun. By resisting the strong German attack, the French Army turned the battle into an attritional one. Refusing to surrender, they held out until the opening of the Anglo–French offensive on the Somme could successfully divert German resources away and relieve pressure on the besieged garrisons. **Q 23892**

The balance of power had already been changing in noticeable ways with the BEF's expansion in size on the Western Front and more dominant role in operations, but the Somme would be their first opportunity to play such a leading part.

At Verdun, however, the fighting continued. As the wet weather departed with the first signs of the hot summer to come, the strategically important Fort Vaux was captured by the Germans on 7 June, but the battle had by now lost direction and it was difficult to see how either side could establish a clear victory. A final desperate attempt by the Germans was made on 23 June, involving a bombardment of gas shells containing the deadly new phosgene mixture, but it was too late to make much difference. The following day the British and French artillery bombardment had opened on the Somme much further to the west, and the Germans therefore switched to a policy of 'aggressive defence'. The departure of many of the German guns to the Somme sector gave dominance to the French artillery, and Fort Vaux was recaptured on 2 November, followed by a French advance of nearly 2 miles on 15 December. The final casualties of the battle amounted to some 330,000 Germans and 377,000 French.

RECRUITING FOR THE SOMME: THE PALS BATTALIONS

Ellen Parton

On 5 August 1914, the day following Britain's declaration of war against Germany, Field Marshal Lord Kitchener was appointed as the new Secretary of State for War. A respected and popular figure, he would prove instrumental in mobilising Britain for a war which he believed would not be 'over by Christmas' as other principal military and political figures had publicly assumed, but which was likely to last for several years. Kitchener predicted that a protracted and costly war would quickly overwhelm the British Army and, two days after dispatching the British Expeditionary Force to France, he set about creating what was to become the largest volunteer army the country had ever seen.

On 7 August he made a personal appeal to all those 'who have the safety of our Empire at heart' to enlist. The appeal was intended to encourage 100,000 men to come forward, but instead some 500,000 enthusiastically responded. These volunteers would form what was to become known as Kitchener's Army.

Perhaps the most iconic and memorable embodiment of this call to arms was the poster featuring Kitchener's steely gaze and pointed finger. Rowland Luther, who would ultimately serve as a Royal Field Artillery despatch rider during the first day of the Battle of the Somme, recalled the effect of this poster on his own conscience as he enlisted in September 1914:

Huge posters appeared on the hoardings, with a picture of Lord Kitchener, with a finger pointing directly at the onlooker, and the caption: 'I WANT YOU.' Then other posters appeared, of depleted ranks of soldiers, artillery gunners and drivers with empty saddles, urging 'HERE IS A PLACE FOR YOU. FILL IT.' Very inviting indeed...

The famous Kitchener poster was only published in September 1914 and not widely circulated until the following month, after the greatest rush of enlistment had occurred. There were, however, other factors that had encouraged half a million men to volunteer to fight for their country.

Patriotism and a sense of duty were undoubtedly a huge motivator. Horace Astin, who would see service with the 4th Battalion The King's (Liverpool Regiment) on the Somme, remembered the moment he decided to enlist. 'I felt,' he recalled, 'like a lot of patriotic people felt in those days, that Germany was against us and we wanted to do something about it and that we were doing the right thing'. In 1914, Britain had the world's largest Empire and relied upon a formidable Royal Navy in order to control it.

Opposite This recruitment poster, bearing the commanding image of Lord Kitchener, remains one of the most famous images from the First World War and has since become firmly embedded in popular culture. The illustration, by Alfred Leete, was originally created for the cover of the 5 September 1914 edition of **London Opinion** magazine. Despite its fame, the poster version was not circulated widely during the early years of the war; other campaigns featuring Kitchener's image were more commonly seen. **Art.IWM PST 2734**

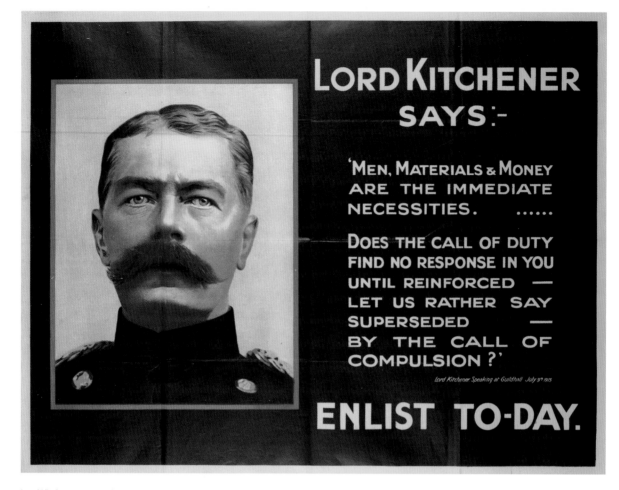

Lord Kitchener was an immensely popular public figure at the beginning of the war and this reputation, combined with his determination to build a larger army comprising new recruits, led to him featuring in numerous recruitment campaigns. This rather wordy example from 1915 relies on his distinguished portrait to sell the message. **Art.IWM PST 11910**

However, jingoistic national superiority and a sense of imperial optimism cannot entirely account for the bellicose atmosphere and rush to the recruiting office in these first few weeks of war.

The population in 1914 was, for the first time, a largely literate one. School was compulsory until the age of 12 and the influence of newspapers and the media was increasingly powerful. In the first few weeks of the war, the press reported only positive news.

However, on 30 August, *The Times* published an accurate and terrifying account of the British Expeditionary Force being forced into retreat following the Battle of Mons:

Our losses are very great... To sum up, the first great German effort has succeeded. We have to face the fact that the British Expeditionary Force, which bore the great weight of the blow, has suffered terrible losses and requires immediate and immense reinforcement.

Kitchener leaving the War Office in London. Having played key roles in the campaigns in Egypt, the Sudan and the Boer Wars, Kitchener held the reputation of a successful senior army officer and colonial administrator. At the outbreak of the First World War, he put considerable effort into raising a new volunteer army to bolster the existing but relatively small British Expeditionary Force. Three days after this image was taken Lord Kitchener was dead. Having accepted an invitation to head a military mission to Russia, he was on board HMS *Hampshire* on 5 June 1916 when she struck a mine off the Orkney Islands. **Q 56658**

STEP INTO YOUR PLACE

PUBLISHED BY THE PARLIAMENTARY RECRUITING COMMITTEE, LONDON ... POSTER Nº 104.   PRINTED BY DAVID ALLEN & SONS L? HARROW, MIDDLESEX. W 2846.. 40 M ~ 10/15

Recruitment drives tended to lay emphasis upon notions of comradeship and community in order to inspire men to enlist. This poster from 1915 makes it clear that the New Army would comprise men from all sorts of different backgrounds, united in a desire to serve their country.
Art.IWM PST 0318

The immediate response to this article was that just four days later, on 3 September, more than 33,000 new volunteers were attested in a single day – more men than usually enlisted in the Army during an entire year.

A sense of adventure and a desire to see the world encouraged many to enlist. It is easy to underestimate the localised nature of Britain at the time, and the opportunity to go abroad (and likely to be back again for Christmas) was an enticing one. Many working-class men had not travelled further than their local town, and this was an opportunity for adventure not to be missed. When considering that they were to be paid (at a time when, economically, many were reduced to working a three-day week) and thus able to provide financially for wives and families at home, whilst at the same time exercising their sense of duty, it becomes easier to see why they were so keen to 'get in before the end of the excitement' as volunteer Joseph Hird put it. Bert Fensom, a salesman, shared this reason behind his own decision to enlist:

The declaration of war offered an escape for me and the possibility of a new outlook on life and I decided to join the forces and take an active part in the fighting... [My firm] accepted my gesture as an act of patriotism, but for me, it was to act for freedom and a new outlook on life.

The War Office was overwhelmed as men lined up for hours at local recruitment offices and town halls to enlist. Britain had no systematic contingency plans for mass enlistment and so relied upon local authorities, industrialists and committees of private citizens to offer assistance. Consequently, it was often down to MPs, local businessmen, sports clubs and even churches to lend or hire out halls where doctors could provide the often cursory medical examinations and facilitate the processing of the new recruits.

Reports of under-age and medically unfit men successfully passing through the pressured system are common. Schoolmaster John Beeken joined the

Leeds Pals take the oath of allegiance at Leeds Town Hall in September 1914, in the presence of their Commanding Officer, Colonel Walter Stead, and the Lady Mayoress. Within two days of the first call-up, over 1,000 men had joined the battalion which would be officially designated as the 15th Battalion, The Prince of Wales' Own West Yorkshire Regiment. **Q 111825**

10th Battalion East Yorkshire Regiment (the 'Hull Commercials'), along with many of his friends. While confident of his own suitability, he was surprised to witness a comrade, blind in one eye, being passed fit for service:

I watched him anxiously as his sight test came along. He was told to cover up one eye and read the letters on the test card. He covered up the left eye and easily read the letters. When told to cover up the other eye, he calmly covered up the left eye and so passed the sight test. He was declared to be physically fit.

Indeed, family and friends played a unique role in recruiting for Kitchener's Army. It was quickly realised that many more men would enlist if they could serve alongside their friends, relatives and colleagues. United by a sense of loyalty and of mutual experiences, their allegiance to each other, as well as to their country, was a powerful recruitment tool. Men could, in the words

of volunteer George Dale, 'stay together like brothers' on the battlefield. Nearly every parish had some kind of recruiting agent, and local groups tapped the conscience of their neighbours in recruitment drives. On 21 August 1914 the first 'Pals Battalion' began to be raised from the stockbrokers of the City of London. It was the Earl of Derby who made the following appeal, published in Liverpool newspapers on 27 August:

It has been suggested to me that there are many men, such as clerks and others engaged in commercial business, who wish to serve their country and would be willing to enlist in the battalion of Lord Kitchener's New Army if they felt assured that they would be able to serve with their friends and not be put in a battalion with unknown men as their companions.

It was also Lord Derby who first coined the phrase 'Battalion of Pals' at a meeting held at the drill hall in St Anne Street, Liverpool, on 28 August.

By tapping into the civic and community pride of these like-minded men and appealing to their complex local and national identities, he recruited enough men to form three battalions of The King's (Liverpool Regiment) in just one week. Cabinet Minister David Lloyd George named Lord Derby 'the most efficient recruiting sergeant in England', and his influence cannot be overestimated – especially on the communities of northern Britain, including the cities of Manchester, Leeds, Newcastle, Hull, Glasgow and Edinburgh, which became synonymous with the Pals Battalions. Lord Derby would take on the role of Director-General of Recruiting the following year when, in autumn 1915, the so-called Derby Scheme was launched in order to encourage even more men to declare their willingness to enlist, prior to conscription finally being introduced in March 1916.

In two days of the call being put out, over 200 Preston men had formed a company of the 7th Battalion Loyal North Lancashire Regiment, joined by volunteers from Blackpool, Kirkham and Chorley. This enthusiasm was matched by other communities across the (mainly) northern counties. However, Pals Battalions were also raised from Birmingham to Bristol and from Cambridge to Cardiff. The result was that, by the end of September 1915, 50 Pals Battalions were either complete or in the process of formation.

Once attested, the new soldiers had to be moved to training depots where there was often no facility to house them and little opportunity for training. The Pals Battalions fared slightly better than most, as their training depots were often established locally, exploiting local networks and connections. Their raising committees

Above Volunteers for the Preston Pals line up in front of Preston Town Hall during the early months of the war. Within two days of an advertisement being placed in the *Lancashire Daily Post* on 31 August 1914, some 250 local men had volunteered for military service who would go on to form part of the 7th Battalion, The Loyal North Lancashire Regiment. Despite minor involvement in the Battle of Loos, the Preston Pals would suffer their first significant casualties on the Somme, during the fighting for the woods in July and August 1916. **HU 53725**

Opposite Leeds Pals at their training camp on the Yorkshire dales in September 1914. Note that the soldiers are still wearing their own clothes; their pipes were donated by a local benefactor, but proper uniforms did not arrive until November. **Q 111826**

PUBLIC SCHOOLS BRIGADE
ROYAL FUSILIERS
118th INFANTRY BRIGADE

HURRY UP! BOYS
RECRUITING OFFICE
20, WESTMINSTER PALACE GARDENS
WESTMINSTER.S.W.
FILL THE RANKS

Among the Pals were the Public Schools Battalions, made up almost exclusively of former public schoolboys. Most of the early recruits preferred to serve as private soldiers alongside their comrades, but a lack of officers meant that many were encouraged to apply for commissions in other units. Many Public School Pals ended up being posted to the 16th Battalion Middlesex Regiment which saw action on the First Day of the Battle of the Somme as part of the 29th Division's doomed attack on Beaumont Hamel. **Art.IWM PST 0332**

blue serge uniforms were used, informally referred to as 'Kitchener Blues', while old and obsolete uniform was taken out of stores and reissued. In addition, some 1,300,000 jackets and trousers and 900,000 greatcoats were obtained from Canada and the United States. Meanwhile, men improvised with strips of cloth around their arms to identify their unit and in a number of battalions, where uniform but not badges had been issued, brass buttons and customised badges were worn on the men's caps. Soldiers of the Leeds Pals were provided with pipes by a local benefactor upon their enlistment in September 1914, but they were not issued with uniforms until two months later. R E Foulkes described the recruits, visually at least, as resembling 'a rag and bobtail lot', while Reg Bailey commented that his unit's mixed clothing made them look like 'Cossacks'. Major E I Andrews, who would lead his men into action on the first day of the Battle of the Somme, described his own uniform in similarly disparaging terms:

Tactics in the Yeomanry were really relics of the mounted infantry of the Boer War, circa 1900, and some of the equipment dated from that period. My own Great Coat was blue with a red lining and silver buttons and may even have been older than that. Few buttons remained and the material was so old that an additional tear appeared whenever it was handled. This of course always happened before the Kit Replacement Inspection, but even that failed to achieve the desired result, and the horror remained with me until I left the Regiment in 1915.

Equipping the men with weapons and equipment was a similarly protracted affair, and many units were forced to carry out much of their arms training with obsolete or dummy weapons. Initially, whilst the new recruits were being introduced to the discipline and routine of military life, this was not too much of a problem, but it was to have a far-reaching effect on the men's readiness for battle. In his dairy, Private Leonard Salter recorded how he spent a total of four mornings in bayonet practice before being dispatched to France, which was less time than he spent undergoing regular kit and hut inspections. Similarly, Thomas Jennings, who served with the 'Bantams' of the Gloucestershire Regiment in 1915, reflected that, 'We were to cram in, in a few months, all the training and manoeuvres it took the old regular army 18 months to accomplish'.

undertook to both feed and clothe the new soldiers, with local tradesmen engaged in building the depots to house them. Such was their localised nature that, after joining the Pals, some men were even able to return home for evenings and weekends.

Most training depots were ramshackle affairs, established hurriedly in response to the huge influx of new recruits. Their improvised structures were not the only problem, as there were nowhere near enough uniforms for the new recruits. Most men remained in civilian clothes for a number of weeks and, in some cases, months. 500,000 Post Office

Recruits of the Grimsby Chums (later designated the 10th Battalion Lincolnshire Regiment), during rifle training in September 1914. The Grimsby Chums were in the first wave of troops to attack La Boisselle, south of the Albert–Bapaume road, during the First Day of the Somme. They occupied the crater following detonation of the so-called Lochnagar mine, but suffered significant casualties. **Q 53286**

Once their training was complete, the Kitchener Army divisions were sent to France, with most arriving during early 1916 in time for the British attack on the Somme. Of the ten battalions suffering the highest casualties on the first day of the battle, seven were from Kitchener's Army. Of the 500,000 men who responded ot Kitchener's initial call to arms, it was the Pals Battaliions, with their geographical bonds and social grouping, who suffered the most. Entire communities lost their sons, husbands and fathers on the morning of 1 July. Whole districts were in mourning. Jennings wrote that comrades from 'Berkshire plowmen [to] Berkshire artisans' were killed in a matter of a few hours.

In letters written home to his wife shortly before the Battle of the Somme, in which he himself would suffer a mortal wound on the first day, Captain Bill Bland reflected on the comradeship of the men he served with in the Manchester Pals (the 22nd Battalion Manchester Regiment). Even though he had an inkling of what lay ahead, he praised his fellow soldiers' solidarity:

What does it feel like to be on the edge of what may prove to be the mightiest battle waged in the history of the world? Like all romance, it is most unromantic to the participators at the time of participation. The spirit cannot grasp either the facts or the issues, the imagination is at work with the practical possibilities, and the brain is busy with the overload of detail, immediate and prospective. We are all like ants, as they appear to a disturber of their nests, terrifically busy in an apparently purposeless orgy of chaos... [It is] the ties of association that bind one to this and that set of people... The common cause that binds, and common memories, joy, laughter, madness and boredom experienced together. Our Manchester lads are in good form today, burnt brown, eager and keen. I love 'em.

William Orpen, *A Howitzer
in Action*, 1917 (detail).
Art.IWM ART 2957

CHAPTER THREE

BATTLE PLANS

ow that the decision to stage a major Allied offensive on the Somme had been made, planning could continue throughout the beginning of 1916 to the next, more detailed, phase. However, the unexpected German attack on Verdun and resultant drain on French resources meant that the British role would now be the more dominant one in the Anglo–French plan, despite the main direction for the campaign being provided by Joffre. Perhaps unusually, there were no major strategic objectives to the battle, although Haig wrote that he had three clear intentions for the offensive: firstly, to train the divisions and to collect as much ammunition and guns as possible; secondly, to support the French, aiming to take the pressure off Verdun; and thirdly, to improve their positions with a view to making sure that the German forces were beaten during the following year.

The Somme was therefore never intended as 'the battle to end the war', but rather as an offensive to put the British and French in a better position by the end of 1916. While the concept of a Big Push in the summer months was fully expected by all – and undoubtedly intended to be a decisive action in the course of the conflict – it is important to remember that for the British and French High Commands, the Battle of the Somme was always envisioned to be a step towards the end of the war rather than a definite conclusion to it.

With Sir Douglas Haig and his staff now based at their General Headquarters in the chateau at Montreuil, a meeting on 26 May finalised the date of the attack. Joffre insisted that 1 July should be the absolute latest day for the offensive to begin, since the French were suffering under the continued German assault on Verdun and desperately required the pressure on them to be diverted elsewhere. While Haig tried to argue for a later date in August, in order to allow greater time for the British to prepare themselves for such a major attack, this proved unrealistic when faced with the immediate need to support the French. The date of Thursday 29 June was decided upon.

Neither Haig nor his senior officers had previously commanded in battle at the level which would be expected of them for the Somme. The task of carrying out the Somme offensive itself fell chiefly to General Sir Henry Rawlinson's Fourth Army, with General Sir Hubert Gough's Reserve Army being available to exploit any breakthrough. Two divisions of General Sir Edmund Allenby's Third Army would support the attack to the north. Tasked with drawing up the plan of battle, Rawlinson's initial idea was based around the 'bite and hold' tactic of utilizing a fierce artillery barrage to seize the first line of German trenches before pausing to consolidate this new position, then embarking on further attacks. Fearing that early opportunities might be missed before German reinforcements arrived, however, Haig insisted on a deeper initial attack that included at least the enemy's second line. He remained hopeful of a major breakthrough in the German defences, in which case Gough's cavalry would be sent across to fully exploit the situation.

Opposite In this secret memorandum, dated 22 May 1916, Haig asks the Adjutant General, Lieutenant General Sir Nevil Macready, for his view on the most suitable day to begin the Somme offensive. The earliest possible date being considered was 1 July, with the likelihood of the battle actually being launched later. The urgent need to relieve pressure on the French Army defending Verdun meant that the offensive was actually brought forward to 29 June, but in the event this was delayed due to poor weather. **Documents.9506/A**

Secret.

GENERAL HEADQUARTERS,

BRITISH ARMY IN THE FIELD.

A.G.

I have meeting on Friday re best
date for General Offensive with Gen. Joffre.—
Please let me have your estimate
as regards numbers, and reinforcements,
for four dates viz (a) 1st July. —
(b) 15th " —
(c) 1st August.
(d) After middle Aug.—

And state from your point of view,
when we will be in most favourable
position for action,
Yours — D.H.

_____
22 May 16

Another crucial factor dictating the battle plan was the fact that there were still not enough guns to provide the storm-like attack desired by Rawlinson. Instead, a prolonged bombardment would start on 24 June, five days before the main infantry assault, designed to cut the enemy's wire and flatten their defences. Such a long and intense barrage would clearly mean that a good deal of the element of surprise would be lost. The British boasted some 1,010 field artillery guns and howitzers, 182 medium and heavy guns and 245 medium and heavy howitzers – but this was not as impressive as might first be thought, for it equated to one field gun for every 20 yards of trench. At the Battle of Neuve Chapelle in March 1915, the ratio had been one gun for every six yards. The work required of the guns was also more significant than in previous battles, since by now the Germans had adopted a greater number of trench lines, possessed more gun positions and had achieved considerable sophistication in constructing both trenches and underground bunkers. A 'creeping barrage' would be employed to immediately precede the infantry assault, moving slowly forward ahead of the British troops, who would advance at walking pace towards the enemy trenches. This new strategy required a level of sophistication in gunnery skills as yet unproven.

Perhaps the greatest challenge now being faced was the logistical problem of how to move so many men and guns to the Somme sector in readiness for the attack. Captain Harold Yeo succinctly described this immense task in a letter home (written shortly after the battle had begun, due to the immense secrecy surrounding the operation):

The trenches have to be adapted for holding large numbers of men immediately prior to the assault: dumps of food, water, rifle, ammunition, bombs, grenades, and other things have to be prepared so that they can go forward at once [when] success is obtained. I had the job of making those dumps and it was no end of a task. Guns of all shapes and sizes had meanwhile arrived and been put in position; conferences as to orders held; peeps taken from all angles at the promised land.

Nothing on this scale had been attempted before, with the required number of men, horses, guns, shells, food and supplies reaching the millions. Considerable work was needed to create new road and rail links in order to transport material to the Picardy region, while new trenches and gun positions had to be constructed and wells dug for water. Infantry troops out of the line were sometimes called to help with this work, as Private Bernard Stevenson of the 1/7th Battalion Sherwood Foresters complained in a letter home to his mother:

We were only two days in the half-ruined village which is still shelled intermittently but in that brief period I managed to get in the way of one of the most tiring jobs I have ever had the misfortune to meet. We fell in, a party of 50 at 7pm, marched three or four kilometres to where a new railway is being constructed (by the English of course) and there climbed up on the top of trucks full of coal waste or ballast. After a run up the line for another two kilos we were set to work to unload them with shovels. Before the dawn had broken we had disposed of 22 large sized wagon loads, each wagon containing tons of the stuff. Then we had to march back to billets. You never saw such a state as we were in. Faces were black or streaked with dust as any collier fresh from the pit. Indeed there was coal dust in our eyes and ears as well.

Tunnelling activities also began, in order to place mines underneath the German positions for detonation when the attack started. If all of this work was not complicated enough, it was often carried out under enemy fire and in as secret a manner as possible in order not to alert the Germans to the imminent attack. However, such a build-up of military strength could not be hidden completely and the Germans were, of course, fully aware that something ominous was about to happen. Lieutenant Cassel of the 99th Infantry Reserve Regiment of the German Army was present in their front line trenches throughout the months leading up to July 1916 and observed that, 'Day and night we heard trains roll across the valley of the Ancre and speculated what they were transporting. Three months later we should get the answer to our queries'.

Opposite Royal Aircraft Factory F.E.2b two-seat reconnaissance biplane, in flight. Aerial photography and observation came into its own during the First World War as a method of spotting enemy trenches and artillery positions, and studying the effect of bombardments on them. Such preparations for the Somme offensive began many weeks before the scheduled Zero Hour for the infantry attack, with the Royal Flying Corps (RFC) successfully mapping the entire sector by air. **Q 67249**

Indeed, in some sections of the line the Germans were keen to broadcast their knowledge, as Captain Harry Bursey of the Royal Horse Artillery recorded in his diary on 23 June: 'The Huns put a board up yesterday in their front line trenches and on it was pinned a paper with the following: "We know you are going to attack. Kitchener is done. Asquith is done. You are done. We are done. In fact we are all done". Of course they know the attack is taking place.'

Significant new technology for fighting the war would be involved in the Battle of the Somme, with the most prevalent example being the contribution of aircraft. Ever since the start of the war, the Royal Flying Corps (RFC) had been supporting ground troops through their work on photographic reconnaissance and artillery observation. With British troops already based in the Somme sector for some time, the RFC had been busy photographing every part of the enemy lines as a matter of course, allowing intelligence officers the opportunity to identify the German trenches, strong points, headquarters and gun batteries. Aircraft and balloons also provided important guidance to artillery units when calculating their fire. Their position high above the battlefield gave observers a unique perspective, even at night, as Eric Blore of No 31 Kite Balloon Section RFC wrote: 'The air is apparently pricked with little bursts of light – rather like a starry sky in which the stars take it in turn to come out for a fraction of a second. Up and down, thousands of feet above the line but still amongst the flashes, float aeroplanes like lonely swallows.'

With artillery bombardments remaining the key to success in any offensive, the use of aircraft and observation balloons to guide them was therefore crucial. This cooperation was very much a developing skill, however, and the Somme would prove to be a baptism of fire for both the RFC and artillery. During the final days of June, several bombing raids were organised in order to hit rear areas behind the German lines that were unreachable by even the longest-range British guns. The deteriorating weather had led to the date of the offensive being put back slightly to 1 July, but the RFC missions were still to be flown despite the dangerous conditions, as Captain Harold Wyllie of No 23 Squadron RFC recorded in his diary:

Left the ground at 08.25 to bomb railhead and do fighting patrol for two hours round Rovay. Got into cloud at 4,000. Climbed through it to 9,000. Gave it up after two hours during which time I hardly saw the ground and only one of the machines. Nearly had a head-on collision in a thick white cloud. Studd passed me about 10 yards distance. I saw him, or the silhouette of him, tear past at 140 miles an hour. He had one wing very much down, which just saved us as his machine was turning.

Opposite Gunners of the Royal Garrison Artillery in the process of moving an 8-inch Howitzer Mark V into position at Becordel in July 1916. Howitzers of this kind were operated by RGA siege batteries and, despite a reputation for unreliability and difficult maintenance, such guns were considered a very successful artillery weapon for pounding the enemy's positions. **Q 795**

A British 9.2-inch rail-mounted gun shown bombarding German positions. It was one of 467 heavy guns and howitzers located behind the Fourth Army's front by the end of June 1916, which would contribute to the massive artillery bombardment beginning on 24 June. It was the greatest ongoing bombardment of the war so far. **Q 98**

All of this preparation was designed to facilitate the infantry assault, which itself was subject to a great deal of planning and training. Captain George McGowan, signals officer to the 90th Infantry Brigade, described in a letter written shortly before the battle how impressed he was with the degree of preparation:

> When I got back from leave a fortnight ago I was amazed to see what rapid strides have been made in preparation for a struggle, that when I left the line to go on leave, I and many others believed could not possibly take place before August, but where there's a will there's always a way and the powers that be suddenly decided to hustle things. The roads leading to the front line were packed from early morning to early evening with transport stretching for miles back, bringing ammunition and stores. Working parties were hard at it day and night trench digging, cable burying, laying water pipes, digging gun pits and dugouts and carrying out scores of other fatigues necessary to ensure success. After I got back we had a week amongst such turmoil, then we as a brigade left the line by train for the training area. There is a large area here, mapped out with trenches, representing no man's land, the Boche trenches beyond, and a plan of the village of Montauban, which we are to capture and hold, all to scale as obtained by aerial photographs. Trenches, streets, etc. are marked with names that we shall christen them when we get across there, and here the Brigade goes en bloc each day, to practise step by step (in accordance with the timetable fixed for the actual day) our part in the big offensive.

Empty 18-pounder shell cases, just part of the total fired by one British division in the bombardment of Fricourt before the attack of 1 July 1916. Of the wounds inflicted on British soldiers throughout the First World War, over half were caused by shells and mortars. As the Battle of the Somme progressed, the British artillery began to learn the value of concentrated fire to keep the enemy in their dugouts as opposed to more widespread destructive bombardments. **Q 113**

The preliminary artillery barrage, intended to destroy the German defences that had been identified by the RFC reconnaissance flights over the previous months, opened in the early morning of Saturday 24 June. The noise from the guns would have been deafening. As Corporal George Ashurst of the 1st Battalion Lancashire Fusiliers recalled, it was hard to believe that anyone could survive such an intense barrage:

> We were just standing looking at the German lines and we could see the bursts of the shells – all over – big ones in the distance. We could see the dirt from the sandbags dancing up and down. Then you could turn about and all along the skyline you would see flashes: big flashes, little flashes, hundreds of them all along the skyline. Over the top there was a roar like a score of trains going all at once over the top of your head, you could hear them whizzing over. I thought, 'This will certainly shift Jerry, he'll never stand up against a thing like this'.

2nd Lieutenant Jocelyn Buxton of the 2nd Battalion Rifle Brigade provided a similarly descriptive account of the artillery bombardment on Pozières, as witnessed on the morning of 25 June:

> Well, all the long period of toil and preparation and vast accumulation of resources has at last come to its consummation. Two days ago at four o'clock in the morning began the bombardment which now and until the day of assault rages with varying intensity along miles of the front on either side. Events will now work out so rapidly that in many ways it is a definite relief that the weeks of waiting and of preparation are behind us. Beginning at 9.30 the artillery began a systematic bombardment of the villages behind the German lines. The first to receive attention was Pozières, our objective in this sector. For ten minutes all possible guns hurled shells on to the place which could be seen among the trees about 3,000 yards away across an intervening dip. It was not long before it was all swathed in brown and yellow smoke. Meanwhile our innumerable trench mortars had been doing persistent work on the German front line and wire. They have unlimited reserves of ammunition and from the rapid-firing 11-pounders they range to huge 200-pound sort of aerial torpedoes; their apparent effort was terrific. On this day the German retaliation was more marked but it came in rapid bursts and not continuously like ours. There were still long intervals when no answer came from them. It is obvious that they are anxious about their supply of ammunition and are waiting to gauge the magnitude of our intent and for the opening of the attack. One can imagine that the German generals opposite are having to think furiously.

The date of the infantry assault would now be Saturday 1 July. The reports received from observers shortly before Zero Hour suggested that the artillery barrage had done its job well, eradicating the German trenches and destroying the barbed wire defences with its hail of shrapnel. Such news was, in any case, academic since it was now much too late to make any significant amendments to the plan. The battle was about to commence.

On the night of 30 June, the thoughts of every British and French soldier in the sector would have been occupied by their possible fate the following day. Signaller Dudley Meneaud-Lissenburg of the 147th Brigade Royal Field Artillery observed the atmosphere in the trenches, with some writing letters, others conversing in hushed tones and some attempting to make jokes: 'The anxiety, though brave attempts were made to hide it, was clearly discernible on the faces of those seated in silent contemplation of tomorrow, and the pathos of it all overwhelmed me and I found it hard to disguise my emotions.'

Nervously anticipating the morning when his battalion, the 16th Middlesex Regiment, would march out into no man's land, the young subaltern Eric Heaton had already hastily scribbled a letter home to his parents, to be opened only in the event of his death:

The German trenches near La Boisselle seen under bombardment shortly before the British infantry assault. Located on the main Albert–Bapaume road, La Boiselle and the adjacent village of Ovillers were the objectives of III Corps on 1 July, but the artillery's failure to destroy the deep German dugouts resulted in over 11,000 casualties. **Q 23**

I am writing this on the eve of my first great action. Tomorrow we go to the attack in the greatest battle the British Army has ever fought. I cannot quite express my feelings on this night and I cannot tell if it is God's Will that I shall come through – but if I fall in battle then I have no regrets save for my loved ones I leave behind. It is a great cause and I came out willingly to serve my King and Country. My greatest concern is that I may have the courage and determination necessary to lead my platoon well.

No one had such parents as you have been to me, giving me such splendid opportunities and always thinking of my welfare at great self-sacrifice to yourselves. My life has been full of faults but I have tried at all times to live as a man and thus to follow the example of my father. This life abroad has taught me many things, chiefly the fine character of the British Race to put up with hardships with wonderful cheerfulness. How I have learnt to love my men. My great aim has been to win their respect, which I trust I have accomplished and hope that when the time comes I shall not fail them.

If I fall do not let things be black for you. Be cheerful and you will be living then always to my memory. I thank you for my brothers and sisters who have all been very much to me.

Well I cannot write more now. You are all in my thoughts as I enter this first battle. May God go with me. With all my love to you all.

Cheer up,
Your loving Son, Eric.

Zero Hour for the attack would be 7.30am. Along with so many of his comrades on that fine Saturday morning, Eric Heaton would be killed in action.

A wounded man of the 29th Division being brought in across the sunken road at Beaumont Hamel after the assault on 1 July 1916. Many British troops were shot down in no man's land by German machine-gunners based on the dominant Redan Ridge, with survivors then being caught up in the enemy's artillery barrage. **Q 753**

CHAPTER FOUR

THE FIRST DAY

As dawn broke on the morning of Saturday 1 July 1916, the British troops busied themselves with their final preparations before going into battle. Some shared a simple breakfast around 6am shortly before the artillery barrage finally reached its crescendo of ferocity. Many felt optimistic about the forthcoming attack, bolstered by the wide belief that nothing could have survived such an intense shower of explosive metal. While no illusions were held about the harsh fight awaiting the infantry, their first battle objectives should at least be attainable. All shared a strong resolution to 'do their bit', but whether officers, NCOs or the lowliest private soldier, they were all in it together. Major Walter Vignoles, of the 10th Battalion Lincolnshire Regiment, recorded in his diary that the feelings of both himself and his men were overwhelmingly upbeat:

We were in very good spirits; I don't know why, for we all knew that there was a good chance of many of us being killed or wounded, but we were in good spirits and they were not assumed either. Even those who grouse as a rule were cheerful; I think the fact that at last we hoped to get to close quarters with the Boche and defeat him accounted for it. We had an hour to wait, so lighted pipes and cigarettes while the men chatted and laughed, and wondered whether the Boche would wait for us. I had a look round but could not see much. The morning was fine and the sun shining, but the enemy's trenches were veiled in a light mist made worse no doubt by the smoke from the thousands of shells we were pumping into his lines. Nearby I could see our machine-gunners, out in the open already, trying to get the best position from which to enfilade certain parts of the Boche line. There was a kind of suppressed excitement running through all the men as the time for the advance came nearer.

The attack was to be made by 11 divisions of the Fourth Army, positioned in readiness from the north bank of the River Somme to opposite the town of Serre, along with two divisions of the Third Army located further north, opposite Gommecourt. South of the river, five divisions of the French Sixth Army would attack. North of the road running between Albert and Bapaume, the Allied objective was to capture the German first and second line trenches, while south of the road the front line alone was the main aim. Facing them was the German Second Army, commanded by the Prussian General Fritz von Below.

Opposite Soldiers of the 1st Battalion Lancashire Fusiliers fix bayonets prior to the attack on Beaumont Hamel. They are wearing 'fighting order', with a haversack and rolled groundsheet strapped to the belt below the mess-tin which contained rations for two days. The officer in the foreground (right) is wearing an Other Ranks uniform, in order to be less conspicuous to enemy snipers. Featured in the photograph is George Ashurst who, when interviewed by IWM in 1987, recalled how the scene was 'staged' for official photographers a couple of days prior to the actual attack **Q 744**

Everybody knew that the battle's success would be almost completely dependent on the effectiveness of the Allied artillery. The final intelligence and aerial reconnaissance reports had been broadly positive, suggesting that the bombardment had, indeed, done its job – but the only true way of finding out if this was the case would be once the infantry assault was launched at Zero Hour. Since 4am the RFC had been up in the air helping to guide the British bombardment, although the strength of the barrage meant that it was increasingly difficult to identify specific targets or tell which battery was firing at any one time. They also undertook a constant patrol in order to prevent German aircraft interfering with the course of the battle. Lieutenant Sidney Cowan of No 24 Squadron RFC was undertaking this specific duty on 1 July:

> I saw a hostile machine over Péronne and attacked, firing half a drum at about 150 yards. He turned and dived eastwards. When over Pys about ten minutes later, I saw two HA Type A coming west over Bapaume. The other de H's were over Gommecourt. I dived at the hindmost machine and fired half a drum, passed him, and fired the rest of the drum into the other machine. The observer in this machine ceased fire and collapsed into the nacelle, so I climbed up and having changed drums, again attacked the first HA which had attacked me from behind. I fired several bursts into him at close range and he suddenly did a side slip tail slide and fell into a cloud, apparently out of control, and was seen to crash. About five minutes later, while regaining my height somewhere over Achiet-le-Grand, I saw another HA Type C approaching from the north-east. He opened fire at about 400 yards and turned back. I managed to get within about 200 yards and as I was unable to catch him up, fired about 20 rounds. He dived east and I rejoined the patrol.

Meanwhile, the orders circulating down the chain of command to individual officers and infantry units, specifying the objectives they were to capture that morning, were dangerously reliant on a precise timetable. Any deviation from the plan would prove serious. Brigadier General Hubert Rees was in command of the 94th Infantry Brigade:

Opposite A Staff Sergeant (pointing to his right) of the 16th Battalion Middlesex Regiment (29th Division), with a group of troops from the 1st Battalion East Lancashire Regiment, parading at the 'White City' trench opposite Hawthorn Ridge in readiness for the attack on Beaumont Hamel on 1 July 1916. **Q 796**

I was looked upon as something of a heretic for saying that everything had been arranged for except for the unexpected, which usually occurs in war. The short space of time allowed for the capture of each objective made it essential for the whole of my brigade, with the exception of three companies, to advance at Zero Hour, otherwise they would not reach the positions assigned to them at the time laid down. In 20 minutes I had to capture the first 4 lines of trenches in front of Serre. After a check of 20 minutes, I was allowed 40 minutes to capture Serre, a village 800 yards deep, and 20 minutes later to capture an orchard on a knoll 300 yards beyond.

Minutes before Zero Hour at 7.30, mines which had been prepared so carefully by the Royal Engineer tunnelling companies over the last few weeks – deep beneath the German defences, and packed with ammonal explosive – were finally detonated. Secrecy in such operations was essential, as the Germans could be heard digging their own mines close by and the element of surprise had to be maintained at all costs. At 7.20am, the 40,600 lb mine was fired under Hawthorn Ridge in the northern sector between Beaumont Hamel and Serre, while eight minutes later others were detonated near La Boiselle (the 60,000 lb Lochnagar and 40,600 lb 'Y Sap' mines), opposite Fricourt (the Triple Tambour mine), and between Mametz and Montauban (the Kasino Point mine).

However, despite the impressive spectacle they generated, the explosions provided little practical advantage. Their effect was too localised, with German machine guns and artillery in the surrounding areas being moved in quickly to fill the defensive gaps. Indeed, in the case of the Hawthorn Ridge explosion, the Germans were given a good ten-minute warning of the impending assault, allowing them to be poised and ready to meet their attackers, as an anonymous account by a German officer reveals:

There was a terrific explosion which for the moment completely drowned the thunder of the artillery. A great cloud of smoke rose from the trenches of No 9 Company, followed by a tremendous shower of stones, which seemed to fall from the sky all over our position. More than three sections of No 9 Company were blown into the air, and the neighbouring dugouts were broken in and blocked. The ground all round was white with the debris of chalk as if it had been snowing, and a gigantic crater over 50 yards in diameter and some 60 feet deep gaped like an open wound in the side of the hill. This explosion was a signal for the infantry attack, and everyone got ready and stood on the lower steps of the dugouts, rifles in hand, waiting for the bombardment to lift. In a few minutes the shelling ceased and we rushed up the steps and out into the crater positions. Ahead of us wave after wave of British troops were crawling out of their trenches and coming forward towards us at a walk, their bayonets glistening in the sun.

Photograph showing the exact moment when the huge mine dug under Hawthorn Redoubt, containing 40,000 lbs of ammonal, was detonated at 7.20am on 1 July 1916. Located near Beaumont Hamel to the far left of the Fourth Army front, the explosion resulted in a crater some 130 feet across by 58 feet deep. The infantry assault followed ten minutes later at Zero Hour. Q 754

W P.
28.6.16.
673

Dear Else,
Thanks for a chit of some length & liveliness. I think you can put a good deal of faith in what Mrs Pollard says about the end of the War.

As I write the shells are fairly having over; you know one gets just sort of bemused after a few million, still it'll be a great experience to tell one's children about.

So long old thing don't worry if you don't hear for a bit.
I'mas happy as anything as ever
Bill

7.30am was marked by the sound of whistles being blown by British officers all along the front line, signalling the start of the infantry assault. The soldiers emerged from their trenches, climbed over the parapet and began to advance, the British artillery having extended the range of their guns to concentrate on the German reserve lines. Army orders had specified that the men should advance at a steady walking pace in long lines, two or three yards apart. Many senior commanders believed that the inexperienced Kitchener's Army men would be unable to cope with more sophisticated tactics, while such a tight formation would ensure that they arrived at the German line at the appropriate time. There was no need for haste, since it was expected that most of the German defences had already been destroyed by the artillery bombardment. Further waves of men followed every hundred yards or so, their purpose being to help overcome any blockages before consolidating the target objectives. Despite some local variations, this plan was chiefly followed – although, in one specific part of the line, a more inventive method of attack was used. Lieutenant Colonel Alfred Irwin, commanding the 8th Battalion East Surrey Regiment, recalled:

> Captain Nevill was commanding B Company, one of our two assaulting companies. A few days before the battle he had come to me with a suggestion that as he and his men were all equally ignorant of what their conduct would be when they got into action, he thought it might be helpful – as he had 400 yards to go and knew that it would be covered by machine-gun fire – if he could furnish each platoon with a football and allow them to kick it forward and follow it. That was the beginning of the idea and I sanctioned that on condition that he and his officers really kept command of the unit and didn't allow it to develop into a rush after the ball, just if a man came across the football he could kick it forward but they mustn't chase after it.

In most cases, however, the British soldiers simply scrambled out of the trenches and advanced at a walking pace towards the German line. Lieutenant William Colyer of the 2nd Battalion Royal Dublin Fusiliers pithily summed up the experience of many of the British troops as they advanced into no man's land:

Here goes. I clamber out of the front of the deep trench by the scaling ladder and face my platoon. I am smoking a cigarette and superficially am serene and cheerful – at least, I hope I appear so. As I give the order to advance a sudden thought occurs to me: will they all obey? This is instantly answered in the affirmative, for they all climb out of the trench and the advance begins. We are on top of the ridge and under direct fire. I am trying not to mind it, but it is impossible. I am wondering unpleasantly whether I shall be killed outright or whether I shall be wounded; and if the latter, which part of me will be hit. A traversing machine gun rips up the ground just in front of us. That's enough for me; we can't remain in this formation. 'Extend by sections!' I shout. The men carry out the movement well. The Bosche artillery and machine guns are terrific. The anticipation of being hit has become so agonising that I can scarcely bear it; I almost wish to God I could be hit and have done with it. I have lost some of my men. I feel an overwhelming desire to swear, to blaspheme, to shout out the wickedest oaths I can think of, but I am much too inarticulate to do anything of the kind. A shell bursts near and I feel the hot blast. It seems to me this is a ghastly failure already.

It soon became clear that the worst scenario had occurred: the artillery bombardment had failed to achieve its objectives. On the left and to the centre of the Allied advance, the German barbed wire was still in place in many areas, battered but intact, while the enemy trenches were still fully functional defensive works. The German troops had taken refuge in their strong underground bunkers and, as the barrage lifted, were able to emerge with both equipment and command structure intact. The British infantry attack met an unexpectedly strong German defence and the result was complete carnage. 2nd Lieutenant Andrews of the 5th Battalion Cheshire Regiment was part of the Third Army attack to the far left of the line, opposite Gommecourt:

Opposite The 103rd (Tyneside Irish) Brigade, part of the 34th Division, seen advancing from the Tara– Usna Line immediately in front of Albert to attack La Boisselle on the morning of 1 July. The 34th Division, with 6,380 casualties, suffered heavier losses than any other division that day. **Q 52**

Insert In an exception to the usual rule of advancing in line at a walking pace, a patrol crawls forward during the attack on the German trenches at Beaumont Hamel on 1 July 1916. The slope of the defenders' hill is clearly visible, as are trees and the grassy condition of the ground. The initial bombardment had been concentrated on the German lines of defence, and so in many places no man's land had remained largely untouched by the shelling. **Q 745**

Opposite Steps leading down to a huge German underground shelter at Bernafay Wood, near Montauban, captured on 3 July 1916. This photograph gives a good idea of the size and depth of many German dugouts on the Somme. Their skillful construction techniques ensured that deep shelters of this kind survived the intense artillery bombardments, allowing German troops to emerge to meet the attacking force. **Q 4307**

Right The standard German machine gun of the First World War, the MG08 was a water-cooled weapon employing the Maxim system of operation. The German Army was well equipped with machine guns and accorded their operators an elite status. This gun was fired from a heavy four-legged 'sledge' mount, which frequently proved difficult to use in the trenches, and a wide variety of extemporized 'trench mounts' were produced. These mounts put MG08 gunners at a disadvantage since they precluded the use of barrage, indirect or overhead fire. **FIR 9151**

At 7.30 I climbed up the ladder and stepped into no man's land. All was confusion or so it seemed to me. Instead of lines of soldiers advancing steadily on their front, there was just a mob who were at least going in the same direction. There was also a lot of smoke about which may have helped but at least it masked the enemy fire. I felt I couldn't go on in this and halted my platoon, but then I saw over on my left George Arthur going on, so I thought I'd better do the same. I remember seeing my first dead body – a bit of a shock the first – but after that you got quite used to them. I discarded my cane. I can't think why I had it with me. I picked up a rifle which was lying about and it was then that I felt a hell of a bang on my shoulder and found myself on the ground. My left arm was useless and I also felt blood running down my leg. My downfall upset the platoon who, with the sergeant, gathered round me. However, as there must have been a hell of a battle going on around me (I was barely conscious of it), I felt the platoon should get on with the job. I told the sergeant to take the men on to their objective and never mind me. This they did and I am afraid most of them were either killed or captured. I never saw any of them again.

The attack at Gommecourt resulted in only a partial and temporary advance south of the village. Further along the line to the right, the X Corps attack fizzled out despite some success from the 36th (Ulster) Division, who seized the Schwaben Redoubt but were forced to withdraw because of a lack of progress on their flanks. The III Corps attack situated on either side of the Albert–Bapaume road was the worst disaster, resulting in the largest number of divisional casualties that day. Lieutenant Alfred Bundy was serving with the 2nd Battalion Middlesex Regiment, part of the 8th Division advance towards Pozières:

Went over the top at 7.30am after what seemed an interminable period of terrible apprehension. Our artillery seemed to increase in intensity and the German guns opened up on no man's land. The din was deafening, the fumes choking and visibility limited owing to the dust and clouds caused by exploding shells. It was a veritable inferno. I was momentarily expecting to be blown to pieces. My platoon continued to advance in good order without many casualties and until we had reached nearly halfway to the Boche front line. I saw no sign of life there. Suddenly however an appalling rifle and machine-gun fire opened against us and my men commenced to fall. I shouted 'down', but most of those that were still not hit had already taken what cover they could find. I dropped in a shell hole and occasionally attempted to move to my right and left but bullets were forming an impenetrable barrier and exposure of the head meant certain death. None of our men was visible but in all directions came pitiful groans and cries of pain. I began to suffer thirst for my water bottle had been pierced with a bullet. After what seemed hours of waiting I was almost tempted to take a chance and crawl back in daylight. I was dreading the dark for I thought I should lose my sense of direction in my distraught condition. I finally decided to wait till dusk and about 9.30 I started to crawl flat on my stomach. At times I made short wild dashes and finally came to our wire. The Boche were still traversing our front line trenches and as I lay waiting for strength to rush the final few yards, sparks flew from the wire continuously as it was struck by bullets. At last the firing ceased and after tearing my clothes and flesh on the wire I reached the parapet and fell over into our trench now full of dead and wounded. I found a few of my men but the majority were still out and most were dead. Came across my Company Commander Hunt who was almost insane. Took charge of C Company of about 30 men!

Opposite R. Borlase Smart, *A Dugout*, 1917. **Art.IWM ART 4463**

Casualties were high across all units, but some particular battalions were truly slaughtered: the 10th Battalion of the West Yorkshire Regiment alone lost 710 men of all ranks. German counter-attacks during the afternoon recaptured much of the lost ground north of the road, making fresh British attacks against Thiepval unsuccessful.

Very little ground indeed was taken to the left of the British line, and that which had been captured was achieved at a tremendously high cost. While it would be easy to criticise the British attackers, who in many cases lacked experience and training, insufficient artillery was also a factor. Although shells were now being supplied to the front in high numbers, they were extremely variable in quality. Some shell casings differed in length, leading to their course wavering in flight, while many shells were 'duds' which failed to explode on impact. Some historians have also highlighted the 66 pounds of kit being carried by many of the British troops, which weighed them down, affecting their speed and mobility. As Albert Hurst of the 17th Battalion Manchester Regiment recalled:

Soldiers of the 16th Battalion Middlesex Regiment fall back under heavy fire having reached the crater on Hawthorn Ridge, which is at the centre of the horizon. This photograph was taken at 7.45 am on 1 July 1916. On the first day of the battle the attacks along the northern part of the line were largely repulsed by the Germans, although further south some success was achieved. **Q 755**

Wounded men of the 1st Battalion Lancashire Fusiliers being tended in a trench in the 29th Division's area near Beaumont Hamel on the morning of the initial assault. 19,240 British officers and other ranks were killed while 35,493 were wounded on 1 July. The soldier on the extreme left carries two anti-gas PH helmets in satchels. **Q 739**

We had two extra bandoliers of rifle ammunition, a rifle as well as Mills bombs in two of our pockets, a full-sized pick, panniers of Lewis-gun ammunition in water buckets. Men were carrying barbed wire, posts for the barbed wire to go on, cutters for barbed wire. Every man had some extra load. We had to put up barbed wire and dig ourselves in when we got there. You could just about walk. On the back of our packs we had a blank metal plate to reflect the light so that the aeroplanes could see how far we had got in our advancement.

Such heavy packs were not used all along the line, however. Some units chose to discard any unnecessary equipment before attacking, based on the experience and common-sense of individual officers.

Rather than being seen as just a failure on the part of the British, a fairer précis of the situation would draw attention to the notable strength of the German defences. The Germans had learned significantly from the previous year's fighting, and had made considerable advances in the design and construction of bunkers and strong points that protected them during the British bombardment. Once the barrage lifted, both men and guns emerged to wreak havoc on their attackers. Lieutenant Cassel, a German officer of the 99th Infantry Reserve Regiment, was among the front line defenders as the X Corps moved on Thiepval:

More than a week we had lived with the deafening noise of the battle, and we knew that this went on not only in our sector but northwards almost as far as Arras and southwards as far as Péronne. Dull and apathetic we were lying in our dugouts, secluded from life but prepared to defend ourselves whatever the cost. The shout of our sentry, 'They are coming!' tore me out of my apathy. Helmet, belt, rifle and up the steps. On one of the steps something white and bloody, in the trench a headless body. The sentry had lost his life from a last shell, before the fire was directed to the rear – he had paid for his vigilance with his life. We rushed to the ramparts; there they come, the khaki-yellows, they are not more than 20 metres in front of our trench. They slowly advance, full equipped, to march across our bodies into the open country. But no, boys, we are still alive – the moles come out of their holes. Machine-gun fire tears holes in their rows. They discover our presence – throw themselves on the ground, in front of our trenches. They are welcomed by hand grenades and gunfire, and now have to sell their lives themselves.

Meanwhile, to the south, on the other side of the Albert–Bapaume road, results were somewhat more successful as the Fourth Army troops attacked the villages of Fricourt and Mametz. The configuration of the front line there, which ran at an angle in front of the British-held Maricourt Ridge, allowed good observation over the German trenches and permitted enfilade fire by artillery units, supported by French guns in the neighbouring sector. Significant damage was done to the German artillery and their wire was effectively cut, leaving little to threaten the British infantry of the 18th and 30th Divisions who advanced and soon captured the village of Montauban. Captain Nevill, along with the football-kicking 8th East Surreys, was with the 18th Division who achieved their immediate objectives despite high casualties. Nevill himself was killed in the attack. Nearby, 2nd Lieutenant George Ellenberger's 9th Battalion King's Own Yorkshire Light Infantry were part of the attack towards Fricourt:

Photographs taken on the afternoon of 1 July 1916. In the first (main), taken at about 3.30pm, soldiers of the 7th Battalion The Queen's Regiment and the 7th Battalion The Buffs (Royal East Kent Regiment) are on the Montauban Road before their final advance on Montauban Alley. The officers seen are Lieutenants C A Haggard and D R Heaton, with an officer of the 7th Buffs. The subsequent photograph (inset) shows the same men in the successfully captured Montauban Alley trench, the final objective of the 55th Brigade, which was taken at about 6.00pm that day.

HU 112461, HU 112462

Above The ruins of Mametz village, captured by the British 7th Division on 1 July 1916. This photograph was taken three days after the initial assault and shows the damage caused by days of constant artillery fire. The Fourth Army saw greatest success around this part of the line at the very beginning of the Somme campaign. **Q 772**

Opposite Roll Call of the 2nd Battalion Seaforth Highlanders on the afternoon of 1 July 1916, near Beaumont Hamel. The insignia on their uniform sleeves indicate that they were part of the attacking force of the 10th Infantry Brigade, 4th Division in VIII Corps. VIII Corps as a whole lost 14,000 men on the first day of the battle to 1,214 German casualties. The tall figure with a notebook but lacking a rifle (in the middle of the image to the left of the NCO who is conducting the roll call) has potentially been identified as the cameraman Geoffrey Malins, who is known to have filmed this scene. **Q 746**

When we had advanced about 20 yards into no man's land we were greeted by a hail of machine-gun and rifle bullets; the Boches had manned the parapet, and when we got near enough they also threw bombs at us: how it was I wasn't hit I don't know. As soon as we reached his trench it was all up with the Hun; we had a regular running fight across his first system of trenches, which had been frightfully ploughed up by our artillery, making the going very difficult. The whole thing was so very fast and it was such hot work, that you hadn't time to sit and think over the horrors, but just went on and on, pursued by a decided but unexpressed feeling that you would sooner be anywhere but there. The Huns ran and we took a lot of prisoners; he has very unsporting ideas about fighting, has the Hun; he'll poop away his machine-gun at you, and he'll snipe at you, and he'll throw bombs at you, but as soon as you get to close quarters with the bayonet he puts up his hands and shouts 'Mercy, Kamerad!': how can you be expected to consider fighters of that description as 'comrades'?! I saw lots of Huns and lots of Hun rifles, and it's an absolute fact that none of them had a fixed bayonet — when it came to bayonet work they put up their hands; the bayonets we found afterwards down in their dugouts!! After this running fight we reached, about 8am or soon after, the Sunken Road about 600 or 800 yards behind the German front line. There we stayed for a few hours, consolidating our position, while some of our troops went on another 200 or 300 yards and occupied Crucifix Trench.

Success was also achieved in the French sector to the far right of the line, where an attack by General Emile Fayolle's Sixth Army took the enemy by surprise. The Germans were not expecting an assault of such ferocity by the French, who they presumed were fully occupied at the defence of Verdun. The greater experience of the French soldiers and their larger proportion of heavy guns meant that they were able to achieve a significant advance, capturing many villages before moving on to Herbecourt and Assevillers by late afternoon. Effective German counter-attacks slowed their advance however and, aware that the British were not experiencing such good fortune elsewhere, the French paused in order to consolidate their position. By doing so, they allowed the Germans to retreat and establish a new, stronger defensive line. Indeed, the German defensive plan throughout the day proved to be extremely robust, and the advantage gained from their strong dugouts and unbroken leadership meant that over the following weeks they would be able to make robust counter-attacks, assisted by targeted barrages to prevent British reinforcements from reaching key areas.

And so the first day of the battle ended. That evening, Lieutenant Russell-Jones, commander of the 30th Division Trench Mortar Battery, was able to record in his diary an advance of about one mile in depth along a sector well over three miles wide, including the capture of Fricourt, Mametz and Montauban, as well as the successful operations by the French in their area:

Chain metal dog-collar removed from a French Army dog killed during the Battle of the Somme. It was acquired by Private W A Holmes of the Essex Regiment – injured in the Somme fighting he was invalided home, bringing the collar with him as a keepsake. The 10th Battalion Essex Regiment were attacking Montauban on 1 July 1916, about a mile and a half from the French sector. **EPH 5239**

Am back in Maricourt writing this; after writing my last we endured perfect hell for a couple of hours, shells landing within a few feet of us every few seconds. Then three men came across from the opposite dugout to say it had been blown in and ten men lying buried in it. Not the slightest use trying to dig them out. It would be a day or more's job and they're already dead. One of the men who came across was Davidson, my old servant in England and sometime servant to Watson. He has caught it very badly. He cannot see and has a piece of shell in his chest, which apparently has entered his lungs for he cannot breathe properly poor lad. I very much doubt if he will get over it, and I'm afraid two other of my very best boys are dead in that other dugout. Both my guns were out of action and there was no use in keeping the men up there, so off I went to get medical aid for the many wounded that we'd taken in and to ask the Headquarters Royal Artillery if I might get the men away. Coming down the trenches I was chased by shells all the way, and the wounded passed on the way too horribly mangled for words. What a ghastly business this whole affair is, but on the other hand what a success it has all been. The Boches are simply giving themselves up in hundreds. We've captured Montauban, on our left they've got Mametz and on our right the French have taken Hardecourt. Let us hope we are in sight of the finish. All the Allies are advancing and behind the dark clouds there is just a little ray of sunshine which we trust will mean peace for ourselves, our children, our children's children, aye and even Peace for ever and a day.

But in spite of such optimism, the fact remained that the casualty rate had been dramatically high. On the evening of 1 July, Sergeant Stewart Jordan was sent to guide the London Scottish back to the trenches after their unsuccessful attack against Gommecourt. A group of exhausted soldiers appeared, wearing kilts: 'When I could distinguish them I noticed about a hundred men I suppose and the adjutant was leading them. So I said to him, "Which company is this please?" "Company?" he said. "This is the regiment!" About eight hundred men went over and about one hundred came back.'

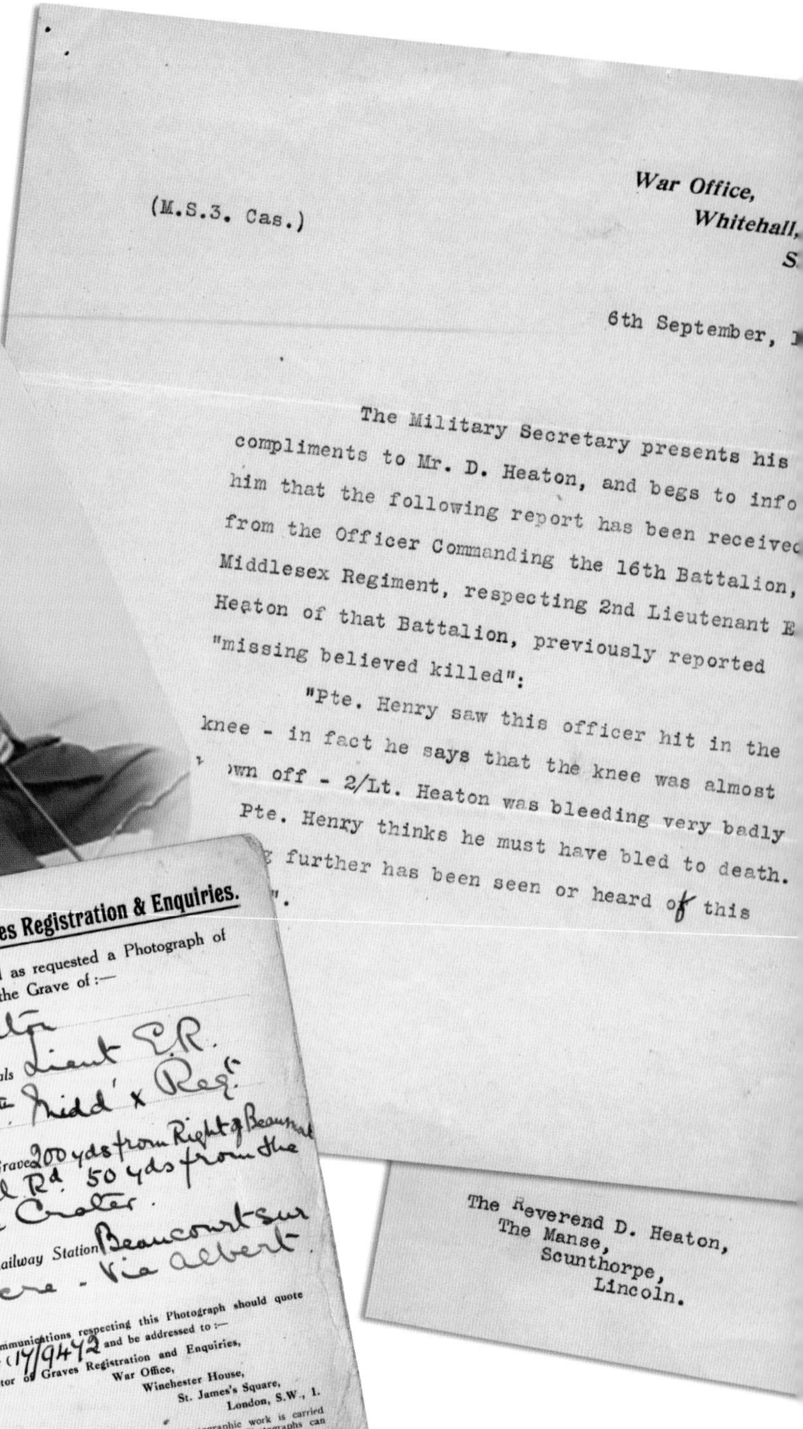

(M.S.3. Cas.)

War Office,

Whitehall,

S.

6th September,

The Military Secretary presents his
compliments to Mr. D. Heaton, and begs to info
him that the following report has been receive
from the Officer Commanding the 16th Battalion,
Middlesex Regiment, respecting 2nd Lieutenant E
Heaton of that Battalion, previously reported
"missing believed killed":

"Pte. Henry saw this officer hit in the
knee - in fact he says that the knee was almost
wn off - 2/Lt. Heaton was bleeding very badly
Pte. Henry thinks he must have bled to death.
g further has been seen or heard of this
".

The Reverend D. Heaton,
The Manse,
Scunthorpe,
Lincoln.

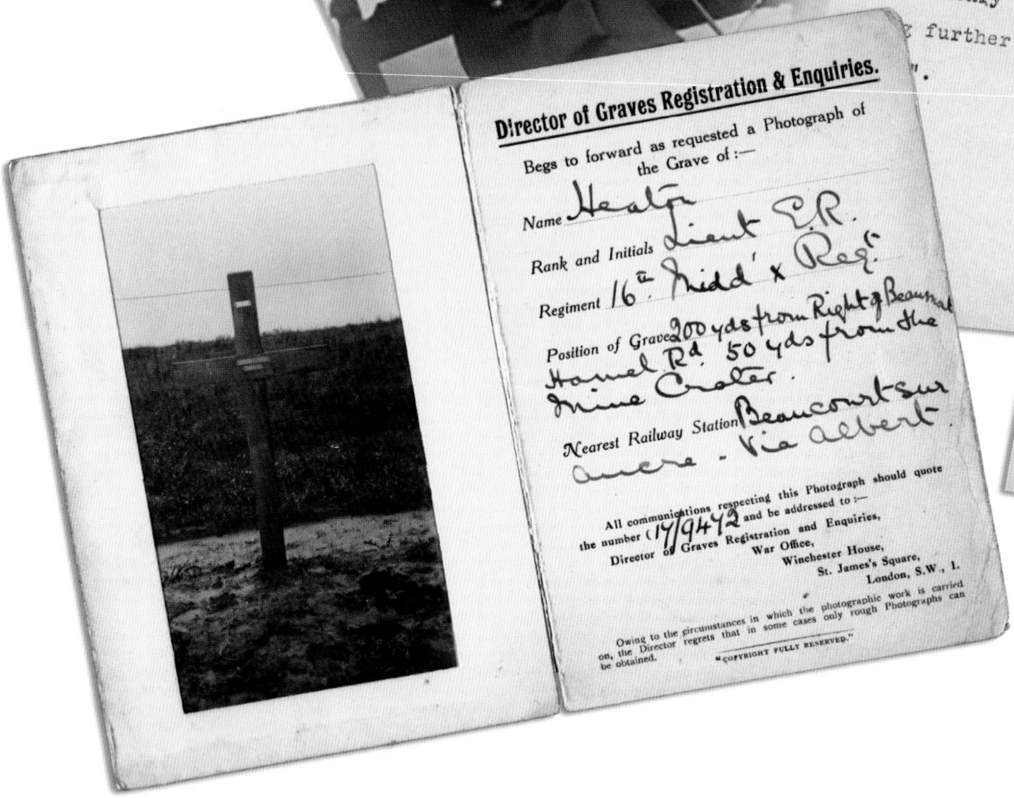

Director of Graves Registration & Enquiries.

Begs to forward as requested a Photograph of
the Grave of :—

Name Heaton

Rank and Initials Lieut E.R.

Regiment 16th Midd'x Regt

Position of Grave 200 yds from Right of Beaumont
Hamel Rd. 50 yds from the
Mine Crater.

Nearest Railway Station Beaucourt-sur-
Ancre - via Albert

All communications respecting this Photograph should quote
the number (1)/9472 and be addressed to :—
Director of Graves Registration and Enquiries,
War Office,
Winchester House,
St. James's Square,
London, S.W. 1.

Owing to the circumstances in which the photographic work is carried
on, the Director regrets that in some cases only rough Photographs can
be obtained. "COPYRIGHT FULLY RESERVED."

The casualty figures speak for themselves: 57,470 British casualties were sustained on 1 July 1916, comprising 35,493 wounded and 19,240 killed. The immediate breakthrough which Haig hoped for had not been achieved, yet information being transmitted back from the front line to the High Command was somewhat mixed. Despite the terrible slaughter to the left of the line, some advance had been made to the right as well as in the French sector. The battle would continue but rather as a more staggered attack which, over time, would become a war of attrition. The massive investment in men and material would not be in vain – the campaign would persist at all costs.

The Director of Graves Registration and Enquiries,
WAR OFFICE,
Winchester House,
St. James's Square,
LONDON, S.W.1.

Director of Graves Registration & Enquiries
14 MAY 1917

...ected to inform you that a report has been
...tes that the late Second Lieutenant E.R. Heaton
...ched 10th Battalion, Middlesex Regiment, is
...00 yards from right of Beaumont Hamel Road and
...rater, Auchonvillers,
...is registered in this office and is marked
...ross with an inscription bearing full

I am,
Sir,
Your obedien...

Captain,
for Brig...
Director G...

N.B.—This Form must accompany any inquiry respecting this Telegram.

POST OFFICE TELEGRAPHS.

If the Receiver of an Inland Telegram doubts its accuracy, he may have it repeated on payment of half the amount originally paid for its transmission, any fraction of 1d. less than ½d. being reckoned as ½d.; and if it be found that there was any inaccuracy, the amount paid for repetition will be refunded. Special conditions are applicable to the repetition of Foreign Telegrams.

Office of Origin and Service Instructions. Charges to pay

War Office London

Handed in at 10.55 Received here at 1.46

TO Heaton The manse Scunthorpe Lincolns

Deeply regret to inform you that 2 Lieut E. R. Heaton middlesex Regt was reported missing believed killed 1st July the army council express their sympathy – Secy War Office

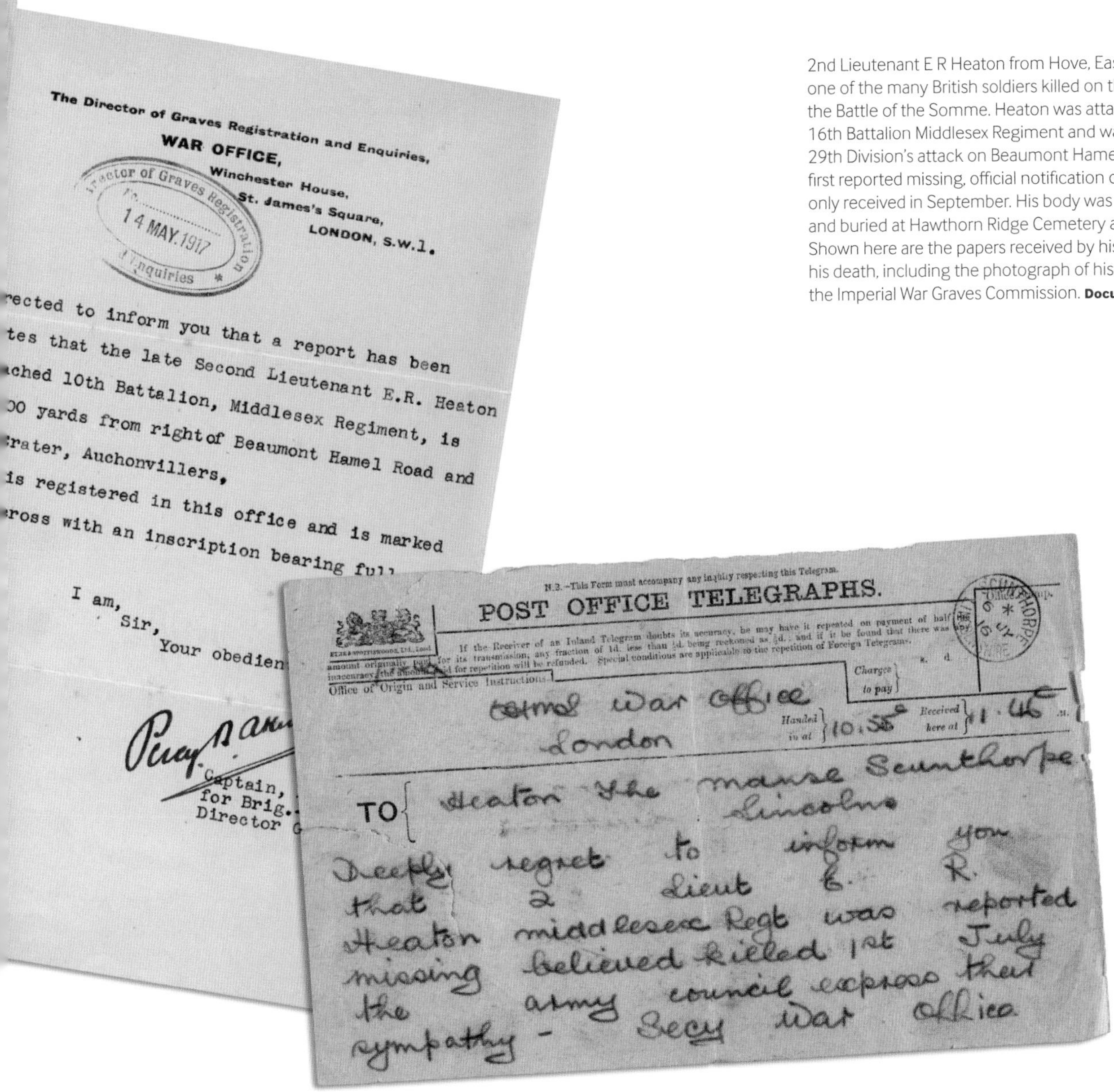

2nd Lieutenant E R Heaton from Hove, East Sussex, was one of the many British soldiers killed on the first day of the Battle of the Somme. Heaton was attached to the 16th Battalion Middlesex Regiment and was part of the 29th Division's attack on Beaumont Hamel on 1 July. At first reported missing, official notification of his death was only received in September. His body was later recovered and buried at Hawthorn Ridge Cemetery at Auchonvillers. Shown here are the papers received by his family following his death, including the photograph of his grave supplied by the Imperial War Graves Commission. **Documents.12701**

Geoffrey Malins was one of the two official cameramen who filmed *The Battle of the Somme*. He is seen here at the extreme right of a photograph showing a visit by William Massey, Prime Minister of New Zealand, to No 8 Squadron RNAS at Vert Galland in October 1916. This image is the only one so far identified that shows the uniform and armband worn by British official 'kinematographers' at this time. **Q 11846**

THE FILM OF THE BATTLE

Roger Smither

London during the past week has been greatly stirred by the public exhibition of the cinema films of *The Battle of the Somme*, shown at 34 theatres and halls. Excellent are the films which show the life immediately behind the trenches, the battalions marching up to the front to go into action, the great guns at their dread work, and the scenes of desolation created by our artillery and by the assaults which drove the Germans from their trenches at places like Fricourt. On a totally different plane, however, is the picture which exhibits the actual attack. ... It would be indeed a cold heart that could resist the thrill of battle that rushes upon one from the shivering screen* (The Spectator, 25 August 1916, p.3).

When the film *The Battle of the Somme* was shown to the press in London on 10 August 1916, just six weeks after the events it recorded and while the battle itself was still a long way from its conclusion, the screening marked the start of a major media phenomenon. The number of people going to see the film in the United Kingdom, the social mix represented in those audiences, and the impression it made on them were all unprecedented. The film had significant impact also as a piece of British propaganda targeted internationally at neutral and allied nations, and even stimulated the making of a cinematic response in Germany. Over the 100 years since it was made, the film has continued to play a major part in determining the manner in which the battle, the Western Front, and the First World War generally have been represented in popular memory. In recognition of its significance, *The Battle of the Somme* was formally inscribed on UNESCO's 'Memory of the World' Register in 2005.

The eventual impact of *The Battle of the Somme* makes it salutary to reflect on the many difficulties – technical, legal and social – that needed to be overcome before such a film could be made. The medium of cinematography was barely 20 years old in 1916, and its technology was still evolving. Cameras were commonly large, heavy machines which needed to be hand-cranked at a steady rate of two turns per second while the operator also managed any camera movement. With the lenses and film stock available at the time, it was difficult to film action in the distance or in the half-light of dusk or dawn, let alone at night. None of this was favourable to filming in combat conditions, although there had been cameramen who were willing to make the attempt and war reporting had been a subject for cinema from its earliest days, the first effort being made during the Greco–Turkish War of 1897.

A more significant obstacle than technical problems was suspicion of the medium among those in authority, on grounds both of security and snobbery.

As arguments for censorship, it was feared that films from the front might reveal military secrets to an enemy or undermine enthusiasm for the war and recruitment at home. At the same time, cinema was a long way from acceptance by the cultural establishment. As popular entertainment it was commonly held in contempt by the traditional arbiters of taste. Lord Kitchener, the Secretary of State for War, had initially prohibited professional film and photography in the front line altogether.

Whatever the official position, however, British cinema audiences were used to seeing current events on the screen – short films described as 'actualities' and 'topicals' had been included from the very first film shows, and compilation newsreel films had spread around the world in the years before 1914. These audiences now wanted to see coverage of the war, and film producers and distributors were happy to cater to their appetite. In the absence of British material, they showed film from the Belgian and French sectors where restrictions on filming were less tight, and some German film even found its way onto British screens. The establishment that had resisted the use of film began to realise that it might be missing a useful opportunity for propaganda, and the War Office agreed to allow the deployment of two experienced cameramen in the autumn of 1915.

The first two 'Official Kinematographers', Edward Tong and Geoffrey Malins, left for the front on 2 November. The material they sent back was presented to the British public as short films in several series of Official Pictures of the British Army in France, the first released in January 1916. Although they were initially received with enthusiasm, a growing body of trade press opinion started to complain that the Official Pictures were insufficiently exciting. The opening of the British offensive on the Somme on 1 July 1916 was to provide an opportunity to silence such criticism.

By this time Tong, who had fallen sick at the end of 1915, had been replaced by J B McDowell, but there were still only two cameramen to cover the entire front of the battle, with the inevitable result that many aspects of the fighting were not covered at all – for example, there is no film of the participation of Irish regiments in the opening of the battle because neither cameraman was in an appropriate location. Nonetheless, Malins and McDowell did manage to cover many aspects of the 'big push' with considerable skill. Almost all of their material was filmed in the two weeks either side of 1 July 1916. The earliest scene is one of the London Scottish, filmed by Malins on 26 June, and the latest shows a Duke of Cornwall's Light Infantry labour battalion filmed, again by Malins, on 8 July. The exception to this pattern is some material specially filmed during a trip to France later in July. (A comprehensive attempt to chart the timing and location of each stage of the two cameramen's work is provided in Fraser, Robertshaw and Roberts 2009, see Sources, page 210.)

Geoffrey Malins initially filmed troop movements and heavy artillery in the area to the west of Gommecourt, at the extreme northern end of the Somme sector, before moving back to the front line via an ammunition dump near Acheux. For the opening of the attack, Malins was formally attached to Major-General H de B de Lisle's 29th Division, and centred his activities on 'White City' facing Beaumont Hamel. From White City he paid an early visit on 1 July to the Sunken Road, halfway across no man's land, held by 1st Lancashire Fusiliers, returning to film the explosion of the great mine under Hawthorn Redoubt and the attack itself. According to his own account he spent the rest of the day filming successive waves of the attack and the return of the wounded and exhausted troops. The next day he 'was told that lively things were happening at La Boisselle' and moved towards the southern end of the Somme front to take further footage there, before returning north and finally travelling back to London on about 9 July.

McDowell, meanwhile, reached the Somme a few days later than Malins, and began filming on 28 or 29 June. He was evidently based further south, filming preparations for the battle to the east of Albert, while his coverage of the events of 1 July and their aftermath was taken largely at positions (notably 'Minden Post') near Carnoy and opposite the Germans at Mametz and Fricourt. Here the attack on 1 July achieved some success, making possible some filming in captured German trenches. These locations suggest that McDowell was also assigned to a specific division, in his case 7th Division, commanded by Major-General H K Watts.

In a still from *The Battle of the Somme*, soldiers of the 1st Battalion Lancashire Fusiliers wait in a sunken lane for the order to attack. Twenty minutes after this scene was filmed, they were under heavy machine gun fire. **IWM FLM 1673**

Still from *The Battle of the Somme*, showing part of a sequence introduced by a caption reading 'British Tommies rescuing a comrade under shell-fire. (This man died 30 minutes after reaching the trenches)'. The scene is generally accepted as having been filmed on 1 July 1916. This image, and the film sequence from which it is derived, has been widely published to evoke the experience of trench warfare, the heroism and suffering of the ordinary soldier, and the huge casualties sustained by the British Army during the initial assault on German lines. In spite of considerable research, the identity of the rescuer remains unconfirmed, although the casualty appears to be wearing the shoulder flash of 29th Division. **Q 79501**

Two stills from *The Battle of the Somme*, showing the moment when the troops go over the top into battle, one man being hit instantly and falling back into the trench. While audiences at the time were shocked to witness such an event captured on film, the sequence is now believed to have been staged at a trench mortar school behind the lines. **Q 70166 and Q 70164**

On its return from France the material shot by Malins and McDowell was recognised as too important for release in the short episode format used for the earlier *Official Pictures*. Instead it was compiled by the American-born film producer Charles Urban, (who had already produced a major factual film with the title *Britain Prepared* in 1915), into a 75-minute feature-length film. As edited by Urban (with some assistance from Malins) the film broadly constructs a story for the battle, starting with preparatory troop movements and the preliminary bombardment, then showing the launching of the attack itself and its effects – prisoners, casualties, captured territory and equipment – before concluding with preparations for further action. The material is not, however, used in a strictly chronological sequence. Some scenes are moved earlier or later to provide more coherence in the development of the apparent story line. The film's most questionable reallocation of a shot is the suggestion that troops filmed before the attack are 'seeking further laurels' after the battle had started.

More notorious than any waywardness in chronology is the film's inclusion of scenes showing troops going over the top that are now universally recognised as having been staged specifically for the camera, probably at a Mortar School near St Pol in mid-July. The inclusion of such material was presumably decided when the rushes were first screened in London on 12 July – it became evident that the genuine footage of troops attacking on 1 July, used in

the finished film immediately after the staged scenes, was not sufficiently clear or impressive to provide a satisfactory visual climax to the film. Awareness of this one example of fabrication has led to a climate where doubt is frequently cast on the authenticity of the rest of the film, or indeed on First World War combat film generally. In fact, however, the majority of *The Battle of the Somme* is genuine, guilty of nothing worse than occasional episodes of direction, when people have been asked to do specifically for the camera something they might well have done anyway.

The Battle of the Somme was a sensational success on its release in August 1916. It has been plausibly calculated that the film had reached 20 million spectators by the start of October and, since it continued to be booked for several more months, that it finally reached the majority of the UK population. Those buying tickets included people who would not usually have gone to the cinema, but seeing the film almost became a patriotic duty. On 6 September *The Times* published an article entitled 'The King And Somme Film', with the King reported as saying, 'The public should see these pictures that they may have some idea of what the army is doing and what it means'.

In truth, the desire to understand the experience of the soldiers at the front would have led people to the film without royal endorsement. At a time when film reviews were not normally carried by the serious press,

Above Still from a sequence in *The Battle of the Somme* captioned as showing 'Royal Field Artillery moving up during battle over ground where the Gordons' and Devons' dead are lying after a glorious and successful charge on the Ridge near Matez'. A limbered-up 18-pounder battery moving over open ground circles round a few corpses, some of which are kilted, as it deploys. The showing of British dead, and the way the war carried on around them, was unprecedented before this film. **Q 79503**

Opposite Still from *The Battle of the Somme* showing a platoon of 'D' Company of the 7th Battalion, Bedfordshire Regiment, passing through a French village on its way to the line. Images like this continued the early cinema tradition of filming groups of people (such as workers leaving a factory) who might be identified by friends and family members visiting the cinema – although the context of wartime introduced the distressing possibility of recognising somebody who was known to have subsequently become a casualty. In this instance the officer at the head of the platoon is Lieutenant Douglas Keep, who was killed in 1917. **Q 79478**

The Battle of the Somme attracted editorial comment across a wide range of major titles. Most of those who wrote about the film said that they felt they were, for the first time, engaging with the reality of the war – on 11 August 1916 people could read of 'The real thing at last' (*Manchester Guardian*), 'A great battle as it really is' (*Daily Express*), and 'War as it really is' (*Daily Sketch*). On 25 August *The Star* wrote, 'It does not reveal all, but what it does reveal is real reality'.

The majority also described themselves as grateful for the opportunity. There were dissenting voices, including those who reflected on the dreadful possibility of recognising on the screen people known to have lost their lives in the battle. Published on 1 September, Hensley Henson, Dean of Durham, famously wrote in a letter to *The Times:* 'I beg leave respectfully to enter a protest against an entertainment which wounds the heart and violates the very sanctities of bereavement', though a large

majority of those who wrote in response firmly defended the film. As Henson's letter also suggested, another strand of opposition to the film came from those who disliked the idea of locating such subject matter in an environment intended for entertainment. This sentiment could cut both ways – according to *The Bioscope* (7 September), one London cinema reportedly displayed a sign reading 'We are not showing *THE BATTLE OF THE SOMME*. This is a place of amusement, not a chamber of horrors'. On the other hand, Frederick Robinson, a civilian too old for military service, noted in his diary on 8 September 1916, 'what people properly take exception to is that these films with all their realism and awfulness should be shewn sandwiched in between screaming farces of the Charley [sic] Chaplin type'. Audiences in general, however, seem to have managed to secure the film-going experience they wanted.

Part of that experience was, of course, that *The Battle of the Somme* was a 'silent' film, though it would not have been viewed in silence – cinemas generally provided musical accompaniment to enhance the atmosphere of spectacle. The absence of sound on film meant that films were interpreted for the audience by captions or intertitles, rather than by a commentary or dialogue. While the captions in *The Battle of the Somme* appear to provide a lot of information, they prove on closer examination to be quite vague and occasionally misleading with regard to places and dates, and never name individuals. For military units, they conform to the normal censorship practice at the time, which allowed the naming of regiments but did not identify the actual fighting units. This approach avoided giving away useful military information, while using the traditional county identification of British regiments to make the sense of involvement as broad as possible. Captions could also be used to prepare the viewer to react in a particular way to a scene which might not automatically provoke such a reaction. Examples in *The Battle of the Somme* include using the words 'thanks to British munition workers' to introduce film of a large munitions dump, or describing German prisoners as 'nerve-shattered' before they are actually seen.

Although *The Battle of the Somme* is sometimes described dismissively as a propaganda film, in fact it carries few such attempts to prompt a desired response to its material. Indeed, some captions – such as those which mention a position coming under enemy fire shortly after it had been filmed, or a casualty dying '30 minutes after reaching the trenches' – might be thought to risk having a negative effect. Propaganda is never an easy weapon to control. Even for a domestic audience, the impact may not be the one that the filmmakers intend. The *Manchester Guardian* editorialised that, 'the more of [war's] trappings that are stripped from it, the more will men see its waste, its madness and its cruelty, as well as its glory, and the more earnestly will they cleave to peace'. An unwanted response could be stimulated even more easily on the international stage. When *The Battle of the Somme* was screened in the neutral Netherlands in September 1916, for example, the *Bioscoop-Courant* wrote: 'This film could serve as an excellent piece of pacifist propaganda, although this may not be exactly the intention of the British Government at the moment'.

Beyond its success on the home front, *The Battle of the Somme* was used extensively overseas, being included in a campaign to demonstrate Britain's commitment to the war effort to her Russian ally, as well as in efforts to sway opinion in Britain's favour in the USA and other neutral countries. Although such efforts were not completely successful, the perception that Britain was taking the lead in the propaganda war led to the creation of a new propaganda agency in Germany in January 1917, the Königliche Bild- und Filmamt (Royal Picture and Film Agency). Among Bufa's first film productions was *Bei unseren Helden an der Somme* (With Our Heroes on the Somme), a specific response to the British film.

Following its impact on domestic and international audiences at the time, *The Battle of the Somme* has become one of the principal sources for the world's visual memory of the First World War. The footage filmed by Malins and McDowell is used extensively, if not always accurately, in virtually every film or television documentary that takes that war as its subject. If *the Battle of the Somme* as an event has an enduring place in collective memory, *The Battle of the Somme* as a film has done much to determine the way it is remembered.

Opposite Poster for the German official film *Bei unseren Helden an der Somme* ('With Our Heroes on the Somme'), which was produced as a response to the international success of the British film *The Battle of the Somme*. **Art.IWM PST 7227**

Casualties from the Battle of Bazentin Ridge. British and German walking wounded, injured in their arms and legs, seen on the way to a dressing station near Bernafay Wood on 19 July 1916. The successful capture of the Ridge was unfortunately not followed up, with reserve troops being released too late and in insufficient strength to capture the next objectives of High Wood and Delville Wood. **Q 800**

CHAPTER FIVE

BAZENTIN RIDGE AND
THE BATTLE FOR THE WOODS

Perhaps out of a desire to quantify and regulate the chaos of war, the first day of the Somme is often seen as distinctive from the rest of the battle. However, for those soldiers who strode into no man's land on 1 July only to end up sheltering from machine-gun fire in ragged shell holes, sometimes lying unconscious, the first day of the battle merged seamlessly into the second. For them, the only matter of importance was how to get back to the safety of their own lines. 17 year-old Cyril José, despite having joined up under-age, had been part of the 2nd Battalion Devonshire Regiment's first attacking wave on 1 July. They were involved in the disastrous assault by III Corps along the Albert–Bapaume road towards Pozières. On entering the battle, Cyril's officer, 2nd Lieutenant Gould, and his batman were immediately shot: 'Both were killed instantly. I jumped to clear them. A bullet thumped through my left shoulder and chest, knocking me down. I panicked and yelled "I'm hit"'.

Against orders, two of Cyril's comrades ran over to him and applied a field dressing to the wound while they crouched some 15 or 20 yards away from the German trenches. Cyril was then left alone, using the bodies of Gould and the batman for cover from the constant bullets and shrapnel. There he lay for the rest

of the day, suffering from intense thirst due to the hot summer sun beating down. Determined not to be taken prisoner by German patrols, he clutched a grenade, ready to pull the pin with his teeth and take any of the enemy with him. Lapsing in and out of consciousness, by 7am the following morning Cyril finally realised that he had to try to get back to the British lines, since he wouldn't be able to survive much longer in his present state:

Slowly I began the long crawl back – the grass was fortunately long. It seemed that I was alone in a field of dead men. The wounded had either made their way back or had been killed in their tracks. Then, about halfway, I encountered Private Lamacraft – a hardened regular soldier, 35 years-old. He was wounded in the back and legs. We struggled along together with my right arm under his body whilst he tried to walk on his hands wheelbarrow-race style. In an hour we had made very little progress. We were both too weak from loss of blood and we had made ourselves conspicuous – Jerry had started firing at us. Luckily, his shooting was very erratic – he too was beginning to feel the strain. I dragged Lammy into a large shell crater and we rested while we took stock. We decided that it was impossible to reach our lines. Lammy had to be carried. There was still a faint chance that I could make it alone. I gathered some water bottles from nearby corpses and stacked them around Lamacraft. Then I set off again, snaking my way through the grass. An eternity later, I spotted a gap in our barbed wire and a sentry's periscope above the parapet. When I drew near enough, I got to my feet and hurled myself into the trench. When I came to, two officers of the Royal Berkshire Regiment were trying to make me swallow some rum. I told them where Lamacraft was and asked them to send out a stretcher party to bring him in. They said it was impossible to send anyone out there. I was taken to a field dressing station, then by lorry ambulance to Bushvillers. Next day I was on a hospital train to Le Treport. All that I remember of the train journey is that it was packed with wounded soldiers. As I could stand, I was in the corridor. In the adjoining carriage, a young Scottish soldier who had lost a leg was singing a song I have never heard before nor since of which the last lines were: 'And, oh, the thought you'll not be mine; Twill break my heart, Margarite, Margarite.'

Opposite Men of the 8th Battalion Border Regiment resting in shallow dugouts in a captured German trench near Thiepval Wood, in a photograph taken around 3 July 1916. Soldiers would frequently have to improvise their living arrangements, adapting existing German dugouts or constructing their own temporary accommodation. **Q 872**

Cyril José would spend the next six months recovering in hospital back in England. The following year, purely by chance, he was reunited with Private Lamacraft who had regained use of his legs but could now only walk with the aid of a stick. He had apparently spent a further three days in no man's land before being rescued.

For those soldiers who had the opportunity, the brief respite following 1 July allowed many to write home in order to let their families and friends know that they were still alive. For those troops still in the line or involved in essential duties, this might involve a hastily scribbled field message postcard to provide basic assurance that the sender was unhurt, while for others more fortunate, a detailed letter home could be composed. Typical of such correspondence written during the first few days of the battle was a letter from Captain Norman Adams of the 6th Battalion South Staffordshire Regiment, recovering from wounds in No 3 General Hospital at Le Treport when he wrote home to his sister:

> I am afraid that we have lost heaps and heaps killed and wounded. Dickinson I heard a rumour of but I pray it isn't true, and little Page, engaged to Jessie Smith, Wilmot Evans, wounded in leg like me, Mayraine broken rib, Evans lost part of his nose and one ear, Robinson blown in the air by shell not wounded but deaf and dumb, Dennis Lewis wounded, Dickens wounded in leg, his third time, Sutcliffe wounded, Hailey wounded in two or three places. Oh, I don't know who else, these I heard of at the various dressing stations on the way here. I expect Reginald is in the bosom of his family by now and really glad to get back if the truth was known.

While in some cases the identity and numbers of dead and wounded could be confirmed immediately, on other occasions there was considerable uncertainty. Many soldiers were still lying out in no man's land, dying from wounds and awaiting recovery, while others had been captured by the Germans and were by now well behind enemy lines. The families of those soldiers in captivity would have to wait for weeks or sometimes even months before definite confirmation was received of their status. In some instances, soldiers went into action never to be seen again, their bodies literally blown to bits by shells or their corpses disfigured to the point where identification was no longer possible.

Opposite The pipe band of the 8th Black Watch playing in Carnoy Valley on 20 July 1916. The 9th (Scottish) Division, of which the battalion formed a part, suffered over 7,500 casualties in the first three weeks of the Somme offensive. Carnoy Valley was full of British dugouts, huts, bivouacs and trenches during the offensive, and was a massing point for British artillery. The Germans knew the importance of the area and shelling was frequent, leading to its nickname of 'Death Valley'. **Q 4002**

On being informed of the 40,000 estimated casualties from the previous day, a figure that was only two thirds of the actual final number, Haig noted: 'This cannot be considered severe in view of the numbers engaged, and the length of front attacked'. The Somme campaign would continue with what is now known as the Battle of Albert, although this was simply a label for a number of smaller, piecemeal attacks intended to improve the tactical positions of the British and French armies in preparation for the next renewed Big Push. There was no question of suspending the offensive while the French were still heavily engaged at Verdun and while the Germans were determined not to give up ground. Falkenhayn had issued clear instructions to the German Second Army on 3 July that they were to fight to recapture lost ground on the Somme at whatever cost. Retreat was not an option.

Gough's Reserve Army was given responsibility north of the Albert–Bapaume road on 2 July, while the line to the south would still be held by Rawlinson's Fourth Army. The Reserve Army initiated attacks on Thiepval and Ovillers in an attempt to gain objectives originally assigned to 1 July, but these soon failed due to the strong German defence. Joffre in particular wanted to push forward in this sector north of the road, where the Schwaben Redoubt beyond the Thiepval front lines would be a prize of significant strategic importance. Haig, however, preferred to exploit existing successes on the far right of the line, to the south. This area in front of Montauban, most prominently the ridge between Bazentin-le-Grand and Longueval, was the favoured direction of any future attack and could also benefit from the involvement of the French Sixth Army, stationed nearby.

This next phase of the offensive to capture the Bazentin Ridge was planned for Friday 14 July. Beforehand, however, it was essential to seize the ground immediately in front, around Contalmaison, Mametz Wood and Trones Wood, in order to establish a strong 'jumping off' point. During the next few days the village of Fricourt, abandoned by the Germans, was taken unopposed by the 17th Division, while German counter-attacks on Montauban were repulsed by the British artillery. Although patrols found Mametz Wood unoccupied on 3 July, they had failed to take advantage of the situation and by the following day it was strongly held once again by the Germans. Between 8 and 12 July, the 38th (Welsh) Division attacked the wood and got within 50 yards of the northern edge before being pulled out, after sustaining some 4,000 casualties. Among their number was Tom Phillips, a Staff Sergeant with the 16th Battalion Royal Welsh Fusiliers:

Opposite RAMC troops carrying wounded soldiers on to a hospital barge at Vaux-sur-Somme, on 25 August 1916. Planning for the evacuation of casualties was essential; such barges were manned by the inland water transport section of the Royal Engineers. With the roads increasingly congested, rivers and canals were the obvious way to transport wounded quickly and smoothly. On 1 August there were 11 such barges operating in France. **Q 4150**

Out of the trench everyone leapt without waiting for definite orders from superior officers. It displayed the instinctive valour of a British Tommy and individual determination to gain the objective. On we went in single file through a heavy Bosch barrage, and on the other side of the crest was a steep embankment which offered the enemy machine-gunners a good field of fire. I do not remember going down this embankment at all as I was so wrapped up in the task allotted to me – I was entrusted with the communications of the 113th Brigade. Our first objective was to get to the Wood and, for the purpose of reorganisation, seek natural cover in the folds of the ground. At this juncture, the enemy put up a heavy barrage of incendiary shells that burst 100 yards or so short. The sudden burst of flame which extended from the point of bursting 200 feet high to the ground had a demoralising effect, as no-one in the Battalion had previously heard of them. Colonel Carden was mortally wounded within 20 yards of the wood. After a brief stay, the troops went forward into the wood… At this point, the Bosch had three machine gun posts which momentarily checked the entrance. These machine-gunners were dealt with. We pressed on until the second objective was reached. I skirted the edge of the wood and ascended the slope till I could be seen by the Brigade forward telephone station and, in doing so, had to dodge the bullets which were fired by snipers up in the trees. I succeeded, with the help of my signallers, to maintain communication during the whole time of this inferno, and the chief messages required to be sent were for more and more stretcher-bearers. The battalion suffered a loss of about 400 casualties in this struggle out of 600 who went into action.

Mametz Wood was finally cleared, and then held by the 62nd Brigade at a cost of another thousand casualties. To its west was located the village of Contalmaison, which commanded the rising ground. On Saturday 8 July, the 1st Battalion Worcestershire Regiment forced their way into the village but had to fall back due to a lack of support. Further attempts led to the 23rd Division successfully capturing the village two days later. By this time the 8th Battalion Green Howards, who had been involved in the attack, had been reduced in strength to only 8 officers and 150 men. Most of the British attacks during this first fortnight of July were characterised by their lack of artillery co-ordination, while the staggered nature of the infantry assaults meant that their overall strength was diluted. Despite the smaller, self-contained nature of these battles, they still resulted in high casualty rates with some 25,000 British casualties being sustained between 2 and 13 July.

Opposite Shrapnel-damaged wallet and pocket book belonging to Lieutenant Robert Stewart Smylie, which he was carrying in his pocket when killed in action on 14 July 1916 during the attack on Bazentin Ridge. The wallet contained a photograph of his wife and their three children. Earlier that morning he had led C Company of the 1st Battalion Royal Scots Fusiliers into position near a quarry to the north of Montauban. When they moved forward onto the slopes of Longueval Ridge, they suffered heavy casualties – five officers were killed, including Smylie.
Documents. 8175

With the finder of this book please send it to Mrs Smylie,
Sudbury Grammar School, Suffolk.

Mon ami, envoyez ce livre à ma femme Mrs Smylie
Sudbury Grammar School Suffolk, Angleterre.

QVI HVNC LIBRVM REPERIET AD VXOREM MEAM
MITTAT. PRO HOSTE IDEM FACERE VELIM.
MRS SMYLIE
SUDBURY GRAMMAR SCHOOL
SUFFOLK, ENGLAND.

"REST"
FROM MY TENT IN FLANDERS
1st R.S.F. 1916

1st Royal Scots Fusiliers,
B.E.F.
Monday 7th Aug.

Dear Mrs Smylie,
I have had it in my mind to write you for some time, but made up my mind to wait till such time as I thought the first rush of your grief would have given place to a softer, if deeper emotion, and a completer understanding.

I hope you have understood, during the past black days, that you have had the sympathy of all the regiment, for nobody was more popular than 'old Smylie' as he was affectionately called: and Tommy Atkins, unimaginative as he is, spent many days discussing and lamenting over old Stewart's little eccentricities & innumerable deeds of kindness.

Speaking personally, it was the hardest blow I have had for the last year: for Stewart and I had been together through days ... and merry days, and I ... myself ... pen and paper ... to me to loose

Mrs Smylie,
Lewisham School Grammar School,
Weston. Super. mare Sudbury
Somerset
Sussex.

Graham

Trones Wood changed hands numerous times throughout six days of harsh fighting. The ground around the wood was considered absolutely essential for launching the planned offensive on 14 July, and so a good deal of worry was expressed by the senior commanders when its capture had not yet been confirmed. At midnight on 13/14 July, a final desperate attempt was made to take the wood, which was only secured after many hours of fighting and 450 casualties. One benefit of having delayed the capture of the wood was that the fighting around Trones served as a distraction to the Fourth Army's main attack.

This would take the form of a dawn assault on Friday 14 July. XIII Corps were to secure German positions on the Bazentin Ridge, between Delville Wood and Bazentin-le-Grand, while XV Corps took the left flank of the attack, aiming for Bazentin-le-Petit and the surrounding woods. To the left of the line, III Corps would offer support towards Pozières. In addition to a three-day heavy bombardment, a five-minute 'hurricane' barrage would precede the infantry attack, which was scheduled for 3.25am. For the first time, the bombardment would consist exclusively of High Explosive, designed to cut the enemy's barbed wire defences. The artillery was learning that a more precise and purposeful barrage was better than simply blasting everything in sight.

With a ratio of one gun to every six yards of front, and against trenches less well-developed than the original front line, the artillery attack proved much more effective than it had done on 1 July. Reginald Perrin was a junior officer commanding a trench mortar battery during the assault:

> A terrific din had been going on for hours, all our guns simply pounding the Hun's front position, and just before Zero this became intensive. If you can imagine more noise coming on top of what one would imagine was the greatest noise possible you have an idea of what it was like. At Zero of course the guns lifted and the front line of the Black Watch followed it at once, followed by all the waves behind. As soon as the line in front of us moved up we got and went forward in our turn. Directly the Hun realised we had started the attack off he went, putting a barrage on our front line trench and behind it to stop any reinforcements coming up, at the same time sweeping no man's land, which was now becoming our land. It has been proved that it is no good bothering about doubling these attacks and they are now taken at a steady walk; so the sight was seen of our men marching over, wave after wave, a square of fire all round, being our barrage in front and the Hun one in rear, also shells bursting in the centre at a lesser rate. The men behaved splendidly, advancing and halting to orders, as if on a field day. Of course the din was too great for them to hear our shouted orders but they obeyed the signs. Anything more exhilarating it would be hard to imagine.

The attack was a great surprise to the Germans, due to the short bombardment and the secrecy with which the infantry had reached their starting positions. Haig still held reservations regarding the inexperience of the troops under his command and had initially forbidden a night approach march and dawn attack, but Rawlinson successfully persuaded him otherwise. By mid-morning some 6,000 yards of the German second line had been captured, with all the objectives gained with the exception of the village of Longueval which, although mostly in British hands, would remain partially contested until the end of the month. The success of the 14 July battle was exactly what the British Army needed after the disaster of 1 July; adversity had been overcome and now momentum needed to be maintained. Lieutenant John Bates, medical officer to the 8th Battalion Black Watch, wrote home to his fiancée on 19 July to tell her the exciting news:

Ever since Friday last we have been in a perfect hell of fighting. We were relieved this morning and thank God I have got out of it safe and sound. We have suffered so many casualties that we are going right away back to refit and reorganise. So you need not be anxious any more. I've been through it and come out safe and sound – how, I don't know. The regiment did simply splendidly and what we have done has been worth the cost. Our battalion led the attack at dawn on Longueval on Friday last July 14th and we have hung on there ever since in spite of incessant artillery bombardment and two strong counter attacks. I went up with the Colonel in the attack and we were heavily shelled on the way up. Got through the Germans' barbed wire all right and found the village practically flattened by our artillery and several fires raging. I can't tell you the whole story now, Girlie, it would take pages and pages, but one day I'll tell you how the house next to my dressing station was blown up by one shell and the barn opposite set on fire simultaneously – how we had to hurry the patients out – how yesterday we were bombarded for seven hours continuously and the concussion in the dugout we were in blew out the candle every minute or so – seven hours of it – from 10am till 5pm we sat in the dugout with shells bursting all around at the rate of about 24 per minute, continuously all the time – how the entrance was half blown in – how the enemy came over right past my dugout but never discovered yours truly and three patients who were inside – how our fellows drove the Hun right back again so that I was able to escape – I will tell you about it all one day and thank God I am safe and sound, out of it, never a scratch. I am going to try and get some leave as soon as possible as it may be easier to get now we are going back to refit than later on. I am absolutely all right and my nerve has not been broken, thank heaven. So I'll see you for certain soon, Girlie – how soon I can't say. I've got two Boche bayonets and a Boche hat as a remembrance of the most exciting, tiring and ghastly five days I have ever spent – at Longueval. In spite of our losses we are all happy and confident.

View of the blasted tree stumps in Delville Wood. On 15 July 1916 the South African Infantry launched an attempt to take 'Devil's Wood', which saw them bravely hold off wave after wave of German counter-attackers. The drawn-out battle would continue for six weeks, with the ground finally being captured on 27 August. This photograph is typical of the scenes of devastation after a major offensive. It took a long time for the forests of France and Belgium to recover from the effects of shells and poison gas. **Q 1259**

Sadly, the successes of 14 July were not exploited. The three cavalry divisions allotted to charge towards High Wood and Martinpuich beyond Bazentin Ridge were released too late and with insufficient strength. The cavalry were faced not only with broken ground, ploughed up by the intense shelling, but also an increasing level of German resistance as reinforcements arrived. Private Anthony Brennan, of the 2nd Battalion Royal Irish Regiment, witnessed their fate:

> We were treated to the stirring sight of a squadron of cavalry going forward on our right. It was, I believe, the first time that cavalry were used on the Western Front since 1914. Anyhow their use on this occasion was somewhat premature and they paid dearly for somebody's blunder. We gave them a cheer as they passed, for we really believed that it was a sign that the breakthrough had come at last. I heard afterwards that most of them left their bones and their horses on the enemy's barbed wire.

In a sense, there was rather too much 'back-seat driving' by the High Command, who over-ruled local commanders. Additional troops kept in reserve and originally intended to exploit any success were deliberately held back in order to repulse potential German counter-attacks. Casualties were again very high. Reginald Perrin's trench mortar battery was called to assist the Argyll and Sutherland Highlanders in the capture of Waterlot Farm:

> This, however, did not come off, owing to the Huns giving the whole place a four-hour bombardment and then counter-attacking, an effort which was duly driven off. During the bombardment we had a very rough time, having practically no cover. My orderly got one shell right on him. I found his head and shoulders lying some distance outside the trench, looking quite peaceful, and his legs inside, all else of the poor fellow had entirely disappeared, but as for plucky deeds, they are too numerous to tell. One chap had both legs blown off and he calmly got out his pull-through, cut it in half, and put a tourniquet on each leg. He was quite conscious as I passed and asked for a drink of water, which I gave him, and sent the stretcher-bearers along. I only hope he pulls through. He deserves to. My casualties are now mounting up.

Despite the successful capture of Bazentin Ridge, albeit at a cost of over 9,000 British casualties, the expected breakthrough had by now degenerated into a long drawn-out battle for the ground in front – most notably High Wood and Delville Wood.

Delville Wood was commonly known by the troops as 'Devil's Wood'. Photographs showing the location during the battle make it clear why it had earned such a nickname. By mid-July, the 156 acres of trees were smashed and in tangled heaps, resembling some kind of twisted, haunted ruin. On Saturday 15 July, the South African Brigade was ordered to take the wood at all costs, despite having lost 92 officers and 2,281 men during the fighting for Longueval the previous day. The Brigade was therefore operating with a greatly reduced 29 officers and 751 men, yet, as Private Percy Robins of their number declared:

> It clearly shows the opinion those in authority have of the South African Infantry that they should have been given the task of clearing the wood... We weren't at it more than ten minutes or maybe fifteen when I got a bullet through the calf of my left leg. Luckily, old Will [his brother] was with me and he put a field dressing on it. I tell you Willie was a perfect Angel of Mercy and a little hero... I'm afraid the censor will not allow me to give you a description of the affair so I will leave that to another time. We've been through a terrible experience and I'm perfectly convinced it was only through God's good grace that we were both spared to come through alive.

The attack began during the early morning and by midday had cleared much of the wood apart from the north-west corner. The enemy made many counter-attacks, all of which were repulsed by the South Africans, while daily attempts to expel the German defenders failed. A massive bombardment was launched on the South Africans on the evening of 17 July, which lasted well into the following afternoon. As the shells rained down, nine German battalions assaulted the wood but were constantly repelled, with the South African Brigade establishing a strong point in the centre of the wood until they were eventually relieved. Fighting continued for a further six weeks before Delville Wood was finally captured on 27 August. As Percy Robins added in his letter home, 'What price the South African Infantry now, eh? They've made a name for themselves but at a sad cost'.

High Wood was unoccupied on the morning of 14 July, but the British missed this opportunity and it would take them another two months to capture the ground. Located on the brow of a hill and at the top of a long open slope, the Germans held the perfect defensive position. Signaller Leonard Ounsworth of the Royal Garrison Artillery was in a forward observation post near High Wood, and so had the perfect location to witness a narrow escape by the 20th Deccan Horse:

Opposite An Army Chaplain takes the name of a wounded man, resting by the side of the Fricourt–Carnoy–Montauban road on 30 July 1916. Chaplains played an important role not only in providing religious support to the troops, but also assisting in the recording of casualties. **Q 4056**

Inset French 400mm railway gun on the Somme. Note how a shell is being moved by a crane to the right of the picture. Such rail-mounted weapons were both very large and immobile, making them vulnerable to enemy attack, and were dependent on the construction of rail links for transport. **Q 49076**

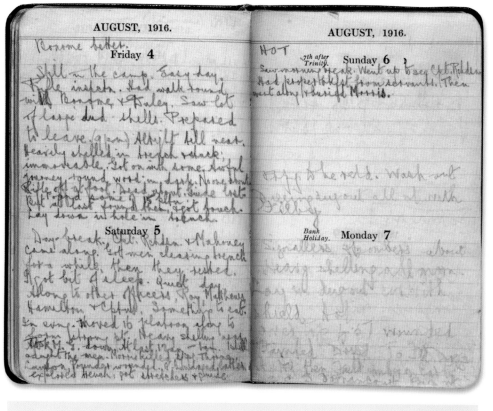

Above 2nd Lieutenant Harold Cope's diary for 4-7 August 1916 records his entry into the line with the 7th Battalion Border Regiment to attack Delville Wood and his subsequent wounding. His battalion took over the eastern half of the wood on 5 August; two days later they were ordered to clear the Germans from their trenches. They tried to cross no man's land but were hit by devastating rifle and machine gun fire. Cope was badly wounded in the right shoulder and immediately lost the use of his arm, with the final diary entry added later and written with his left hand. The attack failed and the wood was not finally cleared until the last week of August.
Documents.14531

Below The 20th Deccan Horse, part of the 2nd Indian Cavalry Division, in Carnoy Valley shortly before their unsuccessful attack at High Wood on the evening of 14 July 1916. Together with the 7th Dragoon Guards, they suffered 102 casualties and lost 130 horses. Despite the successful capture of Bazentin Ridge, the subsequent attempts to seize the woods in front became a long drawn-out battle in the face of strong German resistance. **Q 824**

Opposite Damaged and bloodstained tunic worn by 2nd Lieutenant Harold Cope during the attack on Delville Wood on 7 August 1916. He was so badly wounded that the jacket had to be cut off him before he could receive medical treatment. One of the 6,500 casualties suffered by the 17th Division at Delville Wood, Cope was later evacuated back to Britain for further treatment and recovery. To mark the 50th anniversary of the Somme in 1966, he donated his battle-scarred tunic to the Imperial War Museum. **UNI 10830**

A Morane Saulnier, a French aeroplane that we had at the time, kept diving down on to the corner of the field on our left front. I saw this Indian cavalry, the Deccan Horse they called them, and this plane was diving down and up again. Suddenly the officer in charge of the cavalry cottoned on. He stood up in his stirrups, waved his sword above his head and just charged across that field – like a shot out of a gun, like bats out of hell. The two outer lots split, so they made a pincer and encircled them – it was all over in a matter of seconds. The next thing we saw was 34 Jerry prisoners, some with heavy machine guns. They had been waiting while the cavalry got a bit nearer – my God, they'd have slaughtered them. The plane was trying to draw their attention, just diving down on top – I suppose distracting these machine-gunners, because a plane coming down close above your head is enough to draw your attention.

Above Soldiers of A Company, 11th Battalion Cheshire Regiment, occupy a captured German trench at Ovillers-la-Boisselle on the Somme. One man keeps sentry duty, looking over the parados and using an improvised fire step cut into the back slope of the trench, while his comrades rest. Captured trenches had to be adapted by their new occupants, since they had originally been constructed to defend the opposite direction. **Q 3990**

Below Aerial photograph looking north towards Martinpuich, showing High Wood at the bottom right corner. Aerial reconnaissance of this nature, either by aircraft or balloons, was essential when planning attacks or assessing the effect of artillery barrages. The devastation to the area caused by constant shelling is evident from the landscape. **Q 61359**

In the early hours of 4 August 1916, when repairing broken telephone wires, 27 year-old Lieutenant Alan Lloyd of C Battery, 78th Brigade Royal Field Artillery, was wounded on the Somme by shell-fire. He died within an hour. His signaller, Gunner John Manning from Ancoats in Manchester, was badly shell-shocked but placed a small, handmade marker on Lloyd's grave, and in December 1916 began a moving correspondence with his widow, Dorothy. Lloyd's grave is now in the Commonwealth War Graves Commission's Dartmoor Cemetery at Becordel–Becourt. **Documents.20535**

Concurrent with the fighting to capture the woods, the Fourth Army continued in its attempt to seize Guillemont and Ginchy to the far right of the line, although neither village fell until early September. On the evening of 16 August, 2nd Lieutenant Geoffrey Lillywhite's 9th Battalion East Surrey Regiment were part of the 24th Division attack on German strong-points to the south of Guillemont, which he described in a letter written the following day. Although addressed to his mother, it seems likely that he was aiming his scathing criticism at others back home:

Men of the 2nd Australian Division rest by a roadside on 16 July 1916, during their march to the Somme area to take part in the attack at Pozières. Though British divisions were involved in most phases of the fighting, the attack on Pozières is primarily remembered as an Australian battle. The fighting ended with the Allied forces in possession of the plateau north and east of the village, and in a position to menace the German strongpoint of Thiepval from the rear. However, the cost had been enormous, and in the words of Australian official historian Charles Bean, the Pozières ridge 'is more densely sown with Australian sacrifice than any other place on earth'. **Q 183**

Photograph taken during the official visit by HM King George V to the Somme front in August 1916. On the balustraded terrace of Haig's headquarters at Beauquesne, from left to right, are: General Joseph Joffre (Commander-in-Chief of the French Army), French President Raymond Poincare, HM King George V, General Ferdinand Foch (Commander of the French Army on the Somme), General Sir Douglas Haig (Commander-in-Chief of the British Army). **Q 991**

I should just hope the people are satisfied with what is being done out here! I would give anything for the wretched shysters to see a fine battalion go into action, and then see it crawl out a few days later a shattered wreck, nothing but a handful of men. But those little handfuls are very proud, because they say the same as the Gurkha said, 'If only a few come back they will know we have been fighting'. The Hun realises that in spite of his terrific efforts we are every day snatching back a fresh little piece of his ground. The result is so insignificant on the map, but the cost is heavy. It makes one realise what a hopelessly impossible task it would be to storm the whole line and drive them bodily back. Last night we had a hell of a scrap. Eight officers killed and one wounded and a great number of men also. Many of those killed came from the 11th with me. Still, the job in hand was a big one.

The capture of Guillemont in particular occupied five divisions over a period of almost a month. Attacks by the French Sixth Army throughout July followed the river towards Péronne, gaining a number of important objectives yet at considerable cost and, in some cases, these were subsequently lost to German counter-attacks. By the first two weeks of September, however, greater success was being achieved until poor weather slowed their progress.

While the Germans remained in overall control on the battlefield, this was far from the case in the skies above – the RFC had achieved excellent results in ensuring that the British enjoyed aerial superiority. German scout aircraft were pinned back miles behind their own lines by offensive patrols, leaving the British free to explore above the Somme battlefield as they wished. Lieutenant Eric Routh of No 34 Squadron RFC described his duties:

Diary entry written by Oswald Blows of the Australian Imperial Force. British-born, Blows emigrated to Australia in 1910 and so went to the Somme as an Australian soldier, fighting with the 28th Battalion AIF as part of the 2nd Australian Division. On 23 July 1916 the 1st Australian Division captured Pozières, after four previous British attempts had failed. 2nd Australian Division attempted to continue the advance six days later but, as Blows recorded in his diary, the attack was defeated with heavy casualties. A renewed attempt on 4 August was more successful.
Documents.10798

The principle is for the pilot or observer to get to know the trench system of his own and the enemy area, by direct observation and by the careful study of maps made from photographs, so that he had merely to look at the ground and know it by heart. When the battle is being waged the observer or pilot will watch our troops from above and report their progress or otherwise by message bag to Headquarters... To start with it was found that the staff were somewhat disbelieving, but after a time they learnt to trust us and we were often sent back to make further observations on important points.

By late August, a greater number of German scout aircraft began to appear above the battlefield, and reports were starting to come in of new types of enemy aircraft with a superior performance to those already familiar to the RFC. But, for the moment, the RFC maintained a valuable strategic advantage in the air.

This official German Army issue trench knife was taken as a trophy during the Battle of the Somme by Corporal Mark Lambert of the Bradford Pals, the 16th Battalion West Yorkshire Regiment. On the grip scales he pricked out the word 'Somme', along with his initials. Having spent some time in captivity, he died in Germany in January 1919 before he could be repatriated home. **WEA 3092**

As the fighting for the woods continued, Gough's Reserve Army located north of the Albert–Bapaume road concentrated its efforts on attacking Pozières village, which, from 23 July until 5 August, was the main objective for the Australian Divisions. Pozières would provide an alternative approach to the rear of the German defences around Thiepval, but the village was heavily fortified, having resisted several attacks since 1 July. A night attack launched shortly after midnight on 23 July saw the 1st Australian Division fighting hand-to-hand among the houses and cellars of the town, working their way towards the main road where they dug in. German artillery stopped their advance as they pushed forward, and they were forced to dig in once again. Two days later, the village had been taken at a cost of 5,285 casualties.

The 2nd Australian Division took over and pushed on north in the direction of Thiepval, towards Mouquet Farm. Among their number was Oswald Blows, a British-born Corporal with the 28th Battalion Australian Imperial Force, whose diary entry for 29 July illustrates how their advance had slowed in the face of a strong German resistance:

Above left Daily Telegraph newspaper placard, used in towns and villages throughout Britain, to advertise the latest edition's war news. Although dated 25 August 1916, the attacks on Thiepval were largely redundant until the renewed offensive at the end of September, when the Reserve Army attacked on a wide front in an attempt to capture Thiepval and the important German-held Schwaben Redoubt. The final British objectives would not actually be taken until November. **Art. IWM PST 12968**

Above right Newspapers played a very important role in determining morale on the home front, and invariably concentrated on the positive aspects of the fighting as it progressed overseas. This example from 5 August 1916 stresses the British success, without reference to the correspondingly high casualty figures. **Art. IWM PST 6317**

Our firing line, a captured battered trench, was about 400 yards from the Hun, and our hopping-off trench in front in no man's land. The Hun's trenches were on the ridge almost of a gently rising slope. We were at this time between the wholly ruined Pozières village and the Ridge, our sector taking the road from Albert for Bapaume. The stench was bad from the dead, we'd passed many on our way. We were to make our HQ in a shell hole – 100 yards in rear of [where] our men were to attack, and close to some ruined houses – probably a street once. Arrangements were for our artillery to open up at midnight and bombard until 12.16, then our infantry to rush the first trench, while barrage lifted and bombarded the second line for six minutes, then barrage to lengthen and us to take second trench, and push as far as possible – to make an outpost at least of the ruins of an old windmill near the road. At 12 o'clock our artillery was silent, and us near the Hun's barbed wire, which we had been told was all destroyed. A few minutes past 12 o'clock the Huns began to shrapnel us well, and machine guns were turned on and bombs thrown. A few guns only behind us opened fire, and when our line went forward to the wire they were mown down by enemy machine guns and when the wire was reached, it was almost intact. Our guns opened up more at 12.15, and then some played on the barbed wire and amongst our own men, and what with it, the enemy's artillery (from front and from each side), bombs and machine guns, men dropped in dozens, many on the wire. It was impossible to get through – the barbed barrier was too thick and the enemy being in the know, he put up a living hell. Shell holes were filled with dead, dying and wounded men, and others, and so it was till daybreak, no-one retiring until ordered to do so. The boys all fought gamely and were up against certain death whenever they stood up, and the whole ground was swept with shrapnel. I was in our HQ shell hole, expecting every minute something would catch us. We knew that under the conditions things were a complete failure, and when orders came all that remained of us had to retire – to crawl along to an old trench much battered, and many dead there, both ours and the Hun's. We could not get our wounded in from no man's land owing to the intense fire. Our Battalion went in 1,000 strong and now there is few, if any, more than 300. A few of our men left here a short time ago, and tonight are going to try and bring in our wounded – it was impossible to bring anyone in who could not help himself, and many of our men are still there, poor fellows, with all kinds of broken limbs and wounds. The boys stuck to it bravely and no-one thought of retiring until the order, and officers and men alike showed many a glowing deed.

Further attacks by the Australians led to an advance within 700 yards of Thiepval, yet by then the six weeks of bloody fighting had resulted in a staggering 23,000 Australian casualties, fast approaching the total number lost during the eight-month long Gallipoli campaign. Following a major attack on Friday 4 August, a new front line of trenches was dug which provided a good degree of observation over the village of Courcelette in front and Thiepval Ridge to the left. The scene was thus set for the next Big Push.

On 28 August, an important development in the course of the battle was announced when General Erich von Falkenhayn was dismissed by the Kaiser. Falkenhayn's failure to achieve the promised breakthrough at Verdun was the main cause of his dismissal, with critics arguing that he had drastically underestimated the French strength of arms and determination to fight. The French had cleverly turned the tables on the German Army at Verdun and exploited the war of attrition so that it had worn out their attackers. But intrigue within the German High Command was another contributing factor to Falkenhayn's dismissal. On 29 August, Field Marshal Paul von Hindenburg was appointed as the new Chief of Staff of the German Army, with General Erich von Ludendorff as Quartermaster General but, effectively, Hindenburg's equal in decision-making. Before either man had even visited the Western Front, the Verdun offensive was called off in order to concentrate on defending the Somme.

By the end of August, the course of the Battle of the Somme appeared to be moving slowly but surely towards Britain and France's favour. However, the amount of ground captured was disappointing considering the high cost in men and the time spent in achieving these objectives. In the 62 days from 15 July until 14 September, Fourth Army had advanced 1,000 yards on a 5-mile front, incurring approximately 82,000 casualties. The broader tactical benefits would not always have been immediately apparent to the officers and men who had survived such operations. But by 15 September, a renewed British attack was ready to be launched straight through the centre of the line, with the aim of finally achieving a dramatic breakthrough.

Opposite General Erich Ludendorff (right). Hindenburg, who replaced Falkenhayn as the Chief of the German General Staff on 29 August 1916, acted mainly as a figurehead, allowing Ludendorff to shape much of Germany's military policy. **Q 23746**

BRITISH WAR PHOTOGRAPHY AND THE SOMME

Alan Wakefield

The Battle of the Somme was not only a defining moment in the way the British Army conducted operations on the Western Front, it also proved to be an important turning point in the development of war photography. By the end of the nineteenth century photography had become a popular pastime, fuelled by technical developments pioneered by George Eastman's Kodak company that brought to the public small, lightweight, reliable cameras, using roll film. In 1912 Eastman introduced the Vest Pocket Kodak (VPK), a robust, all metal camera with retractable bellows which, when folded, fitted neatly into a jacket pocket. In Britain competition for Kodak came from manufacturers such as Houghton's, with their folding Ensignette camera. The cost of such equipment, whilst expensive, was not prohibitive, being less than the average weekly wage for a skilled industrial worker.

This growing mass market in camera equipment meant that, with the coming of war in 1914, a not insignificant number of people had cameras with which to document their war experiences. Manufacturers were quick to market their products towards soldiers departing for war. Houghton's stressed how their durable Ensignette was the perfect gift for a loved one heading to the front. In early 1915 Kodak marketed their new Autographic VPK as 'the Soldiers' Camera'. This latest version of their classic design included a metal stylus, allowing short captions to be added to negatives. On developing the negative into a print the caption would be reproduced below the image.

The rise of photography as a hobby coincided with the beginnings of modern photo journalism. The *Daily Mirror*, established in 1904, pioneered this new form of mass media, regularly publishing photographs as part of their news output. Ernest Brooks, William Ivor Castle and William Rider-Rider were among the staff photographers. All three would go on to be British official photographers during the First World War. Newspapers also ran photographic competitions with cash prizes for amateurs. With the coming of war in August 1914 it was obvious that the press would be hungry for images of the conflict. New weekly war news titles such as the War Illustrated were quickly put into production to meet public demand for war news. This development in turn increased the need for photographic images of the war.

Unfortunately, for both the press and public, the armies of the major European powers quickly moved to ban journalists and press photographers on the Western Front, as their work was viewed as a security risk. This forced newspapers and illustrated journals to use photographs supplied by international press agencies. These images often showed French and German troops, and were

Opposite Ernest Brooks, the first British official photographer to be appointed, in a trench on the Western Front. He is carrying a Goerz Anschutz plate camera. Brooks served as a photographer in France and Belgium from March to 1916 to early 1919, while also covering the Dardanelles Campaign in 1915, the Italian Front and naval subjects. After the war he returned to press photography. **Q 24087**

generally taken in the years immediately before the war or behind the lines. Photographs of British troops were restricted to scenes of training in the UK. Action images at this time were mostly dramatic illustrations drawn by artists, of the type familiar to the Victorian audience who had followed nineteenth-century colonial campaigns in the pages of the *London Illustrated News* and other such titles.

This lack of 'real' war images made the press keen to acquire photographs from serving soldiers. The aim was to publish un-posed snapshots taken in the front line. Such photographs would offer an immediacy; capturing a moment in the life of the soldier. On 21 November 1914 the *War Illustrated* published the first British 'in action' photograph of the First World War, showing troops under artillery fire during the Battle of the Marne in September. To meet the increasing demand for such pictures cash prizes were offered for war photographs, with the *Daily Sketch* putting aside a prize pot of £10,000 to encourage and reward soldier photographers.

As increasing numbers of images showing British troops on the Western Front were published, concern within senior military circles grew. Photographs of such events as British and German soldiers fraternising during the 1914 Christmas Truce worked to undermine officially endorsed propaganda messages that increasingly demonised the enemy. In March 1915 a War Office instruction was issued, aimed at banning personal cameras in the British Army. This was reinforced in September that year with the issuing of General Routine Order 1137, which stated that no military personnel or other person subject to military law was permitted to be in possession of a camera. Those disregarding this order were subject to court martial, with officers facing the disgrace of being cashiered from the Army whilst the ordinary soldier faced up to 112 days detention. Yet, despite such punishments, a number of officers and other ranks were still prepared to carry cameras into the front line. One such was Lieutenant Bevis Haggard of the 7th Battalion The Queen's (Royal West Surrey) Regiment, whose two photographs taken on 1 July 1916 (see page 83) during 55th Brigade's successful attack near Montauban are reproduced in this book.

Opposite German photograph showing British prisoners of war at Sailly, in August 1916. Some of the prisoners are clearly wounded, with one standing near the front wearing a bandage around his head, while the German guards herd them together. **Q 45365**

German prisoners captured during the first day of the Somme offensive, 1st July 1916. Official images such as this, showing captured German soldiers, were common throughout the war, as they demonstrated military successes to the readers of newspapers back home. **Q 29**

Although private photographs were still being taken, such images were no longer reaching the public via the press. By the time of the Battle of the Somme, photography, like the printed word, was firmly under the control of the state for propaganda purposes. In March 1916 Ernest Brooks was appointed as the first British official war photographer, given the honorary rank of 2nd Lieutenant and attached to the Intelligence Section of GHQ in France. With his pre-war work for the *Daily Mirror* and experience gained covering the Gallipoli campaign for the Admiralty in 1915, Brooks was the obvious man for the job. During the Battle of the Somme, Brooks was joined by John Warwick Brook, a former photographer for Topical Press. These two men would take the majority of British photographs associated with the battle. The Canadians, too, appointed an official photographer prior to the Somme – Harry Knobel was given the role in April 1916. However, due to ill-health Knobel's service was

short-lived; after just four months he was replaced by Ivor Castle, who had formerly worked with Brooks at the *Daily Mirror*. At the end of the battle in November 1916, Herbert Baldwin arrived on the Western Front to undertake the official photographer's role for Australia.

Britain and her dominions were slow to appreciate the propaganda value of photographs as a medium through which messages could be conveyed at a glance. In Germany, Kaiser Wilhelm II had agreed in August 1914 to the appointment of 19 of his court photographers to cover the war in an official capacity. In September the following year the German Army established a war press office to co-ordinate all types of news and propaganda media. The French, too, organised matters ahead of the British through the formation in April 1915 of the Section Photographique de l'Armée. This branch of the military drew its staff photographers from commercial photo agencies, and took official photographs for

Some of the first wounded British troops of the Somme campaign, pictured here on 1 July 1916. While official photographs of German prisoners were popular, images of wounded soldiers from Britain or its Allies were not so common, for the obvious reason that they would generate worry and criticism back home. **Q 55**

news, propaganda and record purposes. In February 1916 the French established the Maison de la Presse to coordinate wartime propaganda. Within this new organisation's military section lay responsibility for official films and photographs.

In Britain the War Propaganda Bureau was established in August 1914, but initially only dealt with written material. It would be early 1916 before photography was included under its remit. The work of the bureau aimed to create 'the propaganda of the facts' – a phrase coined by its head, Charles Masterman, to convey how it sought to ensure that wartime events were recorded in a way that would not undermine morale. On the whole official photographers followed this line when working, as they were well aware of their duty as part of the national war effort. In addition, as many were pre-war professional photo-journalists, they followed an unwritten ethical code regarding the subject matter of their photographs.

Images of badly wounded or dead soldiers were rare, as such subjects ran counter to accepted levels of decency in Edwardian society. Instead the official photographers took photographs to emphasise the spirit of British and Allied troops, the massed supply of armaments and munitions, and the large number of enemy prisoners. When casualties were depicted these were usually lightly wounded men, shown in the care of the medical services.

The fighting on the Somme stands as a landmark in war reporting, being the first time official photography was used to cover British operations on the Western Front. In the lead up to the opening of the offensive on 1 July 1916, optimism was widespread that the longed-for breakthrough would be achieved. With only Ernest Brooks in place before Zero Hour, GHQ assigned three teams of photographers from the Royal Engineers to supplement his work. Together these men, plus film cameraman Geoffrey Malins, covered the

build-up of British and Empire forces and the week-long preliminary bombardment.

On the morning of 1 July, the photographers were in position at Beaumont Hamel, La Boisselle and Mametz to cover the opening of the offensive. The disaster that unfolded is not reflected in the photographs taken by Brooks and his colleagues. This was due to a combination of factors – the restrictions under which they were operating, lack of numbers (meaning it was only possible to cover a small part of the over 15-miles-long British front over which the attack took place), and limitations of the equipment used. Brooks favoured a standard hand-held Goerz Anschtz press camera. This robust and compact camera took a 5 x 4 inch glass plate negative, which produced a good-sized image for print reproduction. However, the weight of the glass plates meant that, without transport, a photographer could only carry around 24 negatives into the field. In addition none of the cameras in use on 1 July 1916 were capable of being fitted with long lenses. This meant that it was almost impossible to capture the drama of men in action.

Despite such limitations the British press widely featured the photographs, welcoming what was, at the time, a unique and privileged access to the activities of the army in France. On average it took a week for images to reach the newspapers, allowing for censorship at GHQ and in London prior to distribution of the photographs and captions. In terms of early twentieth-century news distribution, this short turn-round time allowed the public to follow wartime events as they unfolded. Even so, as the Somme offensive continued, resources devoted to capturing the events on camera remained limited. The Royal Engineers quickly returned to more pressing military work, which included the taking of panoramic photographs of key sectors of the front line for intelligence purposes. The withdrawal of the engineers left Ernest Brooks and his fellow official photographers to cover the offensive alone.

Opposite Troops of the 4th Battalion Worcestershire Regiment (29th Division) marching to the trenches at Acheux-en-Amiénois on 27 June 1916. The soldiers were evidently asked to cheer by the photographer, although in all likelihood their true feelings about being part of an imminent infantry assault were far from happy. **Q 716**

Signallers spell out the word 'SOMME' using semaphore flags, as they stand in the crater caused by the detonation of the Lochnagar mine. Forbidden to send home information which might reveal their exact location, these soldiers chanced upon a novel way of revealing where they were. **HU 108196**

Despite being few in number, these men were present at each new phase of fighting. They covered the innovative first use of tanks in battle, and documented the relentless five months of fighting that turned large areas of the Somme battlefield into a cratered wilderness.

Just as Brooks and his colleagues used photography to change the way that the British Army at war was documented, so too did the military have its own photographic revolution on the Somme – namely the use of aerial photography as a source of intelligence information. The trench deadlock of late 1914 prevented traditional ground-based methods of reconnaissance, such as cavalry, from seeing what lay behind the enemy front line. Aeroplanes, however, offered armies an elevated, mobile observation platform that could solve this problem. The bringing together of aircraft and photography reinvented how commanders viewed the battlefield. Initially, France led the way in aerial photography, and went to war in 1914 with three specialist photographic sections working with military aviation squadrons. The personnel of these new units were selected for their photographic experience, and worked quickly to develop reliable aerial cameras and mobile darkrooms. Soon the French Army was collating information from aerial photographs into tactical maps and sketches for operational use.

French and British soldiers sharing their rations outside a dugout in Chimpanzee Valley, between Montauban and Maricourt, during September 1916. Allied soldiers in this part of the Somme sector fought closely together, where the part of the line held by the British Fourth Army met that held by the French Sixth Army. The British would learn much from the more experienced French troops. **Q 4203**

Troops of the French 201st Infantry Regiment coming back from the front line in a photograph taken near Bronfay Farm, Bray, on 23 September 1916. The village of Bray was located behind the lines on the River Somme and was part of the French-held sector, serving as an important base for casualties and soldiers on rest out of the line. **Q 67719**

On 13 August 1914 the Royal Flying Corps (RFC) deployed to France in support of the British Expeditionary Force. The RFC took with them five 'Panros' press cameras for aerial photography. In early December the RFC formed No 9 Squadron as a technical development unit to test the use of wireless and photography from aircraft. At the same time officers in No 3 Squadron undertook their own experiments to take aerial photographs. Amongst the personnel involved in these innovations were Lieutenant John Moore-Brabazon and Flight Sergeant Frederick Laws, both pioneer aviators and believers in the value of aerial photography. Learning from their French allies, the RFC established their own photographic sections to which squadrons sent negatives for developing, fixing and printing.

The first major British use of aerial photographs in military planning was during preparations for the Battle of Neuve Chapelle in March 1915. Here, series of aerial photographs were overlapped to form mosaics of the German positions, a technique that quickly became standard practice. The results alerted staff officers to the existence of new German trenches, which led to the modification of the plan of attack. Neuve Chapelle also witnessed the first systematic use of aerial photographs in the production of detailed military maps when combined with survey work of the Royal Engineers. Realising the benefits of this new technology Haig's senior intelligence officer, Brigadier General Sir John Charteris, ensured that from early 1916 aerial photography became an integral part of the BEF's intelligence gathering system. Specially trained photo interpreters were employed to gather a wealth of information from each photograph, and to make this available to headquarters and units.

In preparation for the Somme, the RFC undertook extensive photographic reconnaissance work. Pilots, observers, photographic section staff and photo interpreters worked ceaselessly to keep staff at Fourth Army HQ supplied with up-to-date information on

Mark I 'Male' Tank of 'C' Company, seen broken down while crossing a British trench on its way to attack Thiepval on 25 September 1916. Although providing important support to infantry attacks, the early tanks were liable to break down and conditions for the crews inside were very primitive. **Q 2486**

German defences, artillery positions, troop movements and key locations behind the lines such as transport hubs, camps and depots. RFC squadrons remained active once the offensive began, as each new phase of the battle required aerial photographs to assist with operational planning. By the end of the offensive the RFC had taken 19,000 photographs, from which 430,000 individual prints were produced.

On the Somme the RFC refined the working of its photographic reconnaissance service to a point where new photographic prints could be developed, fixed and delivered to a Corps HQ in as little as 30 minutes following the return of a reconnaissance aircraft to base. Such quick turn-around times provided commanders with fresh and accurate information as fighting progressed. This proved of vital importance, as communications between HQs and the front line were notoriously difficult to maintain, leaving commanders to make decisions based on limited or conflicting information. Having up-to-date photographs on hand

provided a tool to assist commanders in the making of more informed decisions. Maintaining this flow of information was, however, costly. A successful photo-reconnaissance flight called for an aircraft to fly a straight and level course at a fixed altitude and speed. This made the machine vulnerable to enemy ground fire and attack by fighter aircraft. During the Battle of the Somme the RFC lost 308 pilots and 191 observers, killed, wounded or missing.

The personnel of RFC reconnaissance squadrons and the official photographers were severely tested during the Somme. Although under-resourced, they produced significant bodies of work, the usefulness of which was realised by GHQ in France. Images captured by Ernest Brooks and his colleagues, now held by IWM, have for many years been used to illustrate books and documentary programmes. In this way their photographs have become known to a massed audience, and epitomise the collective popular view of the Battle of the Somme and the Western Front.

Shrapnel bursts over Canadian troops in a reserve trench during the fighting near Courcelette, September 1916. At the beginning of September the Canadian Corps of four divisions moved to the Somme and took over from the Australians around Pozières. On 15 September the 2nd and 3rd Canadian Divisions were on the extreme left for the assault on the German third line of defences and successfully captured Courcelette. For the next two months, Canadian units fought almost continually between Courcelette and Grandcourt, capturing formidable German defensive positions such as Regina Trench. The Canadians would suffer 24,000 casualties on the Somme.

CO 802

CHAPTER SIX
FLERS-COURCELETTE

By September 1916, the number of wounded soldiers requiring medical treatment was consistently high. Troops were patched up behind the lines where possible, but those with more serious injuries had to be evacuated back to hospital for surgery and recuperation. Among their number was Private Harold Hayward of the 12th Battalion Gloucestershire Regiment, who had received a bullet wound while serving in the Guillemont sector at the beginning of September 1916. Evacuated back to Lincoln General Hospital, he recalled how the patients would receive regular visits from local well-wishers:

> In this ward there was a lady from one of the county families who used to come once a week. She was rather nosey – wanted to know everything. Her first visit after I was there she said, 'Where was I wounded?' because of course she couldn't see any bandages and I just pointed down under the bedclothes, hoping that would be sufficient. The next week she came she said, 'Where were you wounded?' I knew what she was after and I said 'Guillemont!' It wasn't the particular place she wanted to know but where the wound actually was, which being under the bed clothes she couldn't see. Finally, the next week she pointed and said, 'But where are you wounded?' I was a bit fed up with this continual questioning and so I said, 'Madam, if you'd been wounded where I've been wounded, you wouldn't have been wounded at all!' All the rest of the fellows in the ward guffawed somewhat loudly and she stalked out of the ward not to come back again while I was there.

By now, the Battle of the Somme had turned into a sequence of individual offensives, the time in-between filled by smaller actions designed to straighten the trench line and establish new positions from which to launch the next Big Push. After the fighting around Pozières and the Bazentin Ridge, the next large-scale attempt to break through the German positions would be the Battle of Flers-Courcelette. This offensive involved all three Corps of the Fourth Army and the Canadians of the Reserve Army, assisted by the French Sixth Army to the south. The main aim would be to assault the German third line, creating a gap in their defences between the towns of Morval (located in front of the bitterly contested Delville Wood) and Le Sars (on the Albert–Bapaume road), through which the Cavalry Corps could then advance in order to seize the town of Bapaume.

Opposite Wounded British soldiers at a dressing station set up in the churchyard at Morlancourt, a village well behind the British lines located south of Albert. Note the German bayonet and the Prussian infantry type 'picklehaube' carried by two of the men, which were in all likelihood souvenirs from the recent attack in which they were wounded. **CO 202**

A key factor in the attack would be the first use of a secret weapon built by the British. Sergeant Harold Horne, advancing to the front line in readiness for the attack, was among the first to observe the mysterious addition to their army:

> We passed groups of large objects concealed under camouflage netting, but in the dark could not see what they were. Also we noticed that at intervals white tapes had been laid on the ground leading in the direction of the trenches. When we got into position we had the job of filling in the trench at each place where the tapes met to provide a crossing place. After we got into position, we were told that 'tanks', a kind of armoured vehicle, were coming up to lead the attack.

From very early on in the war, a clear need had been established for an armoured car of some kind in order to cross the uneven ground of no man's land, ride over barbed wire and assault strong-points with its on board weaponry. These unique conditions of the First World War directly influenced the design of the first such vehicles, and the establishment of an Admiralty Landships Committee in February 1915 drew together engineers, manufacturers and representatives from the military in order to construct the initial prototypes. The armoured vehicles were soon christened 'tanks' during production, reflecting their initial similarity to steel water tanks but chiefly to maintain secrecy over their ultimate purpose. The Mark I 'female' tanks carried six machine guns, while the 'male' tanks could be distinguished by their two 6-pounder guns and four machine guns. However, despite numerous trials having been undertaken in secret back in England, it was evident that the vehicles' true capabilities, as well as their inherent drawbacks, would only become clear once they had seen action on the field of battle.

Originally intended to lead the 1 July assault, delays in their production meant that it was not until September that a suitable number of vehicles could be supplied, and this would only be a rather limited 49. In the event, only 36 tanks made their starting positions for the Battle of Flers-Courcelette, in which their objective would be to move ahead of the attacking infantry and assist in suppressing identified strong points.

Opposite British Mark I tank, C-19 'Clan Leslie', shown in Chimpanzee Valley on 15 September 1916, the day that tanks first went into action. Note the net on top of the tank, designed to deflect grenades. A total of 36 tanks reached their starting positions for the offensive on Flers-Courcelette, and trundled into action at their top speed of 4 mph. **Q 5572**

E.C.K. Colla.

MEMORANDA.

Remember your orders.

Shoot quick.

Shoot straight.

Shoot low, because your shot may still hit after ricochet and because a miss which throws dust in the enemy's eyes is better than one which whistles in his ear.

Economise ammunition, and don't kill a man three times.

Remember that trenches are curly and dug-outs deep— look round the corners.

Watch the progress of the fight and neighbouring cars.

Watch your infantry whom you are helping.

Remember the position of your own line.

Smell out the enemy's machine guns and other small guns and destroy them first. They will be cunningly hidden. You must ferret out where they are, judging by the following signs :—

      Sound.

      Dust.

      Smoke.

      A shadow in a parapet.

      A hole in a wall, haystack, rubbish heap, woodstack, pile of bricks.

      They will usually be placed to fire slantways across the front and to shoot along wire.

Use the gun with care ; shoot to hit and not to make a noise.

Never have any gun, even when unloaded, pointing at your own infantry.

It is the unloaded gun that kills the fool's friends.

Never mind the heat.

Never mind the noise.

Never mind the dust.

Think of your pals in the infantry.

Have your mask always handy.

(B 12209) Wt. w.   7960   2000   7/16   H & S   P 16/504

Above Printed 'memoranda' dated July 1916 giving instructions to tank crews. Among the valuable recommendations is the advice that tank crews should 'Never mind the heat. Never mind the noise. Never mind the dust... Have your mask always handy'. Conditions inside the early tanks were very basic, with the cramped space made worse by the deafening noise, poisonous fumes and roasting heat from the engine. The crew of eight Tank Corps men would be working in almost complete darkness with extremely poor visibility. **Documents.21817**

Opposite Muirhead Bone, *Tanks*, c.1917. **Art.IWM ART 2121**

The first tank was sent into action just over an hour before the main attack on Friday 15 September, in order to support a preliminary operation by the 6th Battalion King's Own Yorkshire Light Infantry against a pocket of Germans in the south-east corner of Delville Wood. The Germans, astonished by the appearance of the new weapon, began to surrender before the tank was ultimately disabled by shell-fire.

The main attack launched at 6.20am, following an intense three-day bombardment. The infantry advanced behind a creeping barrage, with tanks accompanying them into battle. In many places the soldiers advanced faster than the tanks, as they kept pace with the moving shell-fire, and the Canadian Corps successfully captured the village of Courcelette. The adjacent town of Martinpuich was taken by the 15th (Scottish) Division with similar success, accompanied by one of the two tanks allotted to them. To the far right of the line, XIV Corps successfully crossed the uncut German wire with the help of their tanks, but were then held up. The Guards Division, ordered to capture Lesboeufs, advanced until they successfully took the German third line trenches.

The main thrust of the offensive and the objective assigned to XV Corps was the village of Flers. As part of the assault, Battery Sergeant Major Douglas Pegler of the 106th Brigade Royal Field Artillery witnessed the infantry making their way towards the German lines:

> Once in the open we could see the infantry struggle up the hill towards Flers, our fellows advancing shell hole by shell hole and the Boche retiring just as slowly and steadily. Whatever Fritz's faults he is a great fighter. Here there is not a yard of ground unbroken by shell-fire and there are half a dozen bodies to each shell hole. When we were through the defile the Colonel gave the order 'Brigade will form line', and then away at the trot, canter and finally mad gallop up the ridge to Flers. The air was thick with shrapnel, and drivers, gunners and horses were going down in all directions, and by the time we got the order 'halt action front' we in my battery had lost 15 drivers, 20 horses and several gunners. By good fortune all the gun teams came through and we were able to get into action.

Some tanks had actually progressed further ahead than the infantry, as described by 2nd Lieutenant Stuart Hastie who was in command of tank D-17:

Opposite A Canadian gunner writes messages with chalk on 15-inch howitzer shells, September 1916. The darkly humorous practice of adding individual messages to shells and bombs was continued by both sides during the Second World War. **CO 766**

Having crossed the front German line I could see the old road down into Flers, which was in a shocking condition having been shelled by both sides. At the other end of this road, about a mile away, which was about the limit of my vision from the tank, I could see the village of Flers, more or less clouded with smoke from the barrage which had come down on top of it and the houses, some of them painted white, some seemed to be all kinds of colours. Across the front of the village, we could see the wire of a trench named Flers Trench and this formed a barricade in front of the village on the British side. We made our way down the remnants of this road with great difficulty. Just as we started off, our steering gear was hit and we resorted to steering by putting on the brake of each track alternately and trying to keep the tank following the line of the Flers-Delville Wood road. When we got down to Flers Trench and passing into the village, there was a great deal of activity from the eaves, under the roofs of the cottages and also from a trench which appeared to be further through the village but which we couldn't just locate at that point. Having steered the engine by using the brakes up to this point, the engine was beginning to knock very badly and it looked as if we wouldn't be fit to carry on very much further ... We went on down through the High Street as far as the first right angle bend. We turned there and the main road goes for a matter of 200–300 yards and then turns another right angle to the left and proceeds out through towards Gueudecourt. But we did not go past that point. At this point we had to make our minds up what to do. The engine was really in such a shocking condition that it was liable to let us down at any moment. So I had a look round, so far as it was possible to do that in the middle of a village being shelled at that time by both sides. I could see no signs of the British Army coming up behind me. So I slewed the tank round with great difficulty on the brakes and came back to Flers Trench and turned the tank again to face the Germans... By this time the infantry did not show any particular anxiety to go on, they were more concerned with consolidating. We made up our minds that nothing could be done with the tank except get it back. We eventually turned the tank off the road to the left, pushed it up against a small hillock which gave us a certain amount of cover – and at that moment the engine packed up and did not start again.

Opposite Mark I tank D-17 surrounded by some of the infantry from 122nd Brigade whom it had led into the eastern part of Flers on 15 September 1916. The photograph was taken two days later. In command of the tank was 2nd Lieutenant Stuart Hastie, who many years later recorded a detailed interview with the Imperial War Museum in which he recalled driving the tank along the main street of the town. **Q 5578**

Opposite Soldiers of the 2nd Auckland Battalion of the New Zealand Expeditionary Force shown in a trench near Flers on 15 September 1916. New Zealand sent more than 100,000 soldiers overseas during the war, and by mid-September the NZEF had taken its place in the centre of the Somme battle line. On 15 September the New Zealand Division successfully attacked between High Wood and Delville Wood, helping to capture Flers, and for a further 23 days it undertook a series of attacks towards Gueudecourt. The New Zealanders suffered around 7,000 casualties, including more than 1,500 dead. **Q 194**

Right The ruins of the main street of Flers after the attack of 15 September 1916. During the advance by the 41st and New Zealand Divisions, tank D-17 attacked through the centre of the village. An aerial reconnaissance report reached XV Corps Headquarters, which read: 'Tank seen in main street Flers going on with large number of troops following it.' This message was later picked up by the press and the wording altered to gain maximum propaganda value: 'A tank is walking along the High Street of Flers with the British Army cheering behind it.' **Q 4271**

Despite the somewhat undignified end to D-17's involvement in the battle, an RFC patrol flying high above the battlefield had sighted the tank trundling through Flers and sent the news back to Headquarters that one of the new vehicles could be seen in the main street, with troops following close behind. With the capture of Flers the German defences were almost broken, but the occupiers were still faced with trouble from enemy reserves who were quickly sent in, and the German artillery who were continuing to pound the village. Meanwhile, in the centre of the line, the 47th Division were advancing on High Wood. At around 8.30am, just over two hours after the battle began, Lieutenant Eric Routh of No 34 Squadron RFC was flying on patrol across the battlefield:

> At High Wood things were not going so well. Just behind the wood a battalion had put out 'XX', denoting 'held up by machine gun fire'. This was immediately taken back and dropped at Railway Copse, the Corps artillery station. Returning, we found the same place had put out 'OO', which means barrage wanted but before we could send it, it was taken in. It therefore remained unsent. The first signal would probably get what was required. The tanks in High Wood were not successful. One had gone over both trenches, rather beyond the Bosche line and there had stuck. It was very heavily shelled for about ten minutes, probably by a trench mortar, so much so that after smouldering for some time it burst into flames. The other two turned over on their side in our own trenches.

The uneven ground and uprooted trees had proved disastrous for the tanks. Trench mortar fire eventually turned the balance of fighting in favour of the British, however, and the wood was finally captured – albeit at a high cost to the 47th Division in terms of casualties, which reached 4,544. Despite his initial scepticism regarding the value of the new armoured vehicles, Lieutenant Routh continued to fly above the length of the battlefront and began to witness the benefits that could be gained from the new vehicles, altering his opinion of their ultimate value:

> Probably a great deal of the day's success has been due to these tanks, they went over five minutes before the infantry and as the Bosche had never seen them before, must have come as the devil of a surprise to them. Another tank engaged a battery just our side of Gueudecourt, it succeeded in knocking out three of the German guns but was knocked out by the fourth. This duel was taking place at about 100 yards. Another tank 'male' and 'relation' got astride of a trench, one at each end and simply wiped out the whole darn crowd. They are great things and have done wonders.

Just over half the number of tanks which trundled into no man's land as part of the main advance had managed to reach the German lines. Many demonstrated success in crushing the barbed wire defences, protecting the British infantry and, perhaps most notably, boosting the morale of the attackers while generating uncertainty amongst the German defence. But they were extremely unreliable, breaking down continually and being too slow to really spearhead any attack, while their crews lacked training and experience. Artillery was still seen as the deciding factor in any attack, with the tank simply a novelty to be fitted in where it could. Despite their limitations, Haig was impressed with the new vehicles and requested that a further thousand be delivered to the Western Front as soon as possible. Due to a lack of skilled workers back home required to construct them, however, production of tanks on such a grand scale would not begin until January 1917. In the meantime, the British would continue to use tanks throughout the Somme offensive but in smaller numbers, as and when they became available.

In many ways the Battle of Flers-Courcelette had been a victory for the Allies, with a considerable amount of the German front line captured and in-roads made into the second line, especially around the town of Flers.

Opposite The remains of a Mark I 'Male' tank of D Company, left abandoned on the battlefield. This tank was probably knocked out during the first tank operation on 15 September 1916. The benefits gained from these early tanks were chiefly psychological in nature, boosting the morale of the attackers and intimidating the enemy. Tactically, however, they offered few advantages with most breaking down or becoming immobilized by the uneven terrain of the battlefield. Only nine tanks actually reached the German lines. **Q 11617**

However, the advance on 15 September was limited to about 2,500 yards on a 3-mile front, and the offensive stalled after the Fourth Army alone had suffered over 29,000 casualties. In order to build on the initial success, however, further attacks were planned in order to seize the objectives of Morval, Lesboeufs and Combles, which had failed to be taken during the initial assault.

Bad weather delayed this renewed attack until Monday 25 September, with Zero Hour scheduled for 12.35pm. For this operation, known as the Battle of Morval, tanks were to remain in reserve. The midday start meant that it would have been difficult to conceal their arrival in the front line, thereby alerting the Germans to the imminent attack. In addition, the main objective for the battle was a more realistic one than in earlier attacks, as the Fourth Army was ordered to capture the German front line only. Private Arthur Russell of the 13th Company Machine Gun Corps was located at the top of a nearby quarry, and so had a perfect view of the attack:

Medals including the Military Cross awarded to 2nd Lieutenant Edward Colle of the Tank Corps for his actions during the tank battle in September 1916. His citation read: 'He fought his Tank with great gallantry, reaching the third objective. Later, on several occasions he went to the assistance of the infantry and finally brought his Tank safely out of action.'
OMD 5445-5451

> We could look across no man's land and follow the movements of both British and French infantry as they streamed across towards the German trenches and the village of Morval. The shells of our dense creeping barrage being placed upon the German positions rushed over our heads with a frightening intensity, but above all that we could hear the humming rushing sound of the thousands of bullets from the eight machine guns of the 13th Machine Gun Company to make that almost impassable barrier between the enemy reserves and their hard-pressed front line troops.

The artillery bombardment was much heavier and more concentrated than before, with greater attention given to targeting German strong points than simply barraging everything. This was very much the 'bite and hold' tactic favoured by Rawlinson as far back as Neuve Chapelle, and the outcome of the operation showed how strong, targeted bombardments and limited objectives could lead to success. The villages of Gueudecourt, Combles and Lesboeufs were all captured by 28 September, with the first two having been largely evacuated by the Germans, allowing the British and French to take both objectives with minimal casualties. An account by Major Harry Dillon, acting commander of the 1st Battalion East Yorkshire Regiment, describes how the Morval operation was a much more slick, planned attack than had previously often been the case:

> After giving them all their orders I shifted with my Adjutant up to the front line and got there about half an hour before the infantry went over. About six minutes before this the barrage started. It was really a wonderful thing – so precise that one might have thought someone had pressed a button. Thousands of screaming shrapnel shells just over our heads and bursting 100 yards in front. At the same time the heavies increased and the whole Hun line about 300 yards off went up in a cloud of dust and debris. Two minutes later our trench, a harmless looking ditch, came to life and as far as I could see (some miles) out came thousands of British soldiers and far away the other side of Combles one could catch the occasional gleam of the French bayonets. It really was a most uncanny sight. They crept out in no man's land, the officers smoking cigarettes and pipes and getting the men into line. Then this line got up and quietly and very slowly marched in perfect line on to the Hun trench, the barrage creeping along in front lifting 50 yards every minute. 50 yards behind a third and then a fourth and almost before one realised it, our front line was in the Germans' trench and streams of Germans were coming back, some wounded but mostly all right. They then put up red flares all along the German trench to show we had got it.

Limited fighting along the front continued with the aim of straightening the line, but on 28 September a request by General Foch led to much of the sector being handed over to French control, allowing them greater manoeuvrability around what was by now a sharply angled salient. With the autumn weather now making itself known, there would be little opportunity left for further offensives before the winter months arrived and the poor condition of the trenches made further attacks too difficult.

William Orpen, *German Wire, Thiepval*, 1917 (detail),
Art.IWM ART 3006

CHAPTER SEVEN

THIEPVAL AND THE ANCRE

H aig continued to believe that the German Army defending the Somme sector was approaching exhaustion. If pressure was maintained, it was hoped, the number of troops at their disposal would run out and their strength as a defensive force would ultimately collapse. Intelligence reports had convinced him that the German reserves were close to being used up and that another hard blow, this time from Gough's Reserve Army, would be enough to make all the difference. While modern critics might suggest that this belief was rather naïve considering the already great sacrifice made in terms of lives lost since the beginning of July, it made sense to the decision-makers of High Command that their enormous investment in men and guns required an equally great return. To call off the offensive with little to show for so many lives would be nothing less than an admission of defeat. Furthermore, the lack of training and inexperience of the British troops at the beginning of the campaign had slowly disappeared as they now began to prove themselves as a professional force. The turning point of the battle was surely approaching.

September's Battle of Flers-Courcelette, despite achieving many of its objectives, had failed to realise the hoped-for breakthrough at the centre of the line. The attention of the battle planners therefore moved north to the other side of the Albert–Bapaume road and the village of Thiepval, beyond which the heavily defended Schwaben Redoubt would prove an important prize. While the Battle of Morval continued at the end of September, Gough's Reserve Army therefore began an attack on the Thiepval Ridge, running from the Schwaben Redoubt to just north of Courcelette.

Zero Hour was set for 12.35pm on Tuesday 26 September. The largest objective was the village of Thiepval itself, which had suffered frequent shelling over the previous three months and was by now a collection of ruins. Originally an objective for the 1 July assault, the area had been the scene of harsh fighting on that day which had resulted in little gain for the British. Nearby was Mouquet Farm, another heap of rubble which had already withstood numerous attacks, chiefly by the Australian divisions following their capture of Pozières and the surrounding ground at the end of July and beginning of August. The task of capturing Mouquet Farm, known as 'Mucky Farm' to the troops, was assigned to the 11th Division. Staff officer 2nd Lieutenant Alan Angus observed the attack:

Opposite William Orpen, *Thiepval*, 1917. **Art.IWM ART 2377**

Trench sign indicating the way to Mouquet Farm. Situated about a mile east of Thiepval, the area was the scene of heavy fighting throughout the period of August to September 1916. More commonly known as 'Mucky Farm' to the troops, it was much fought over with particular involvement by the Australians and Canadians; the location changed hands several times before it was finally captured by the 11th Division on 26 September as part of the larger assault on Thiepval and the Schwaben Redoubt. **FEQ 314**

Two aerial photographs of the German defences at Mouquet Farm, near Thiepval, showing the devastating effects of artillery bombardments between 25 April and 16 September 1916. The farm was one of a number of strongpoints chosen for defence by the Germans, having large underground dugouts and tunnels which made its capture particularly difficult. **Q 27637 and Q 27639**

I was housed in a small dugout about a quarter of a mile behind the jumping-off trench. I had a periscope from inside the dugout to above ground level, and it was thought I would be able to obtain a good view of our whole front and report progress to brigade headquarters. It was known that the Germans had machine guns and mortars in the dugouts beneath the farm, and two tanks were allotted to us for the purpose of mopping up while the infantry went straight on up the hill. The tanks had to remain under cover about a mile behind the farm until zero hour. It was a bright sunny day when, promptly at 12.35, our barrage opened up and our men swarmed out of their trenches and began walking up the hill. The German response was very quick and I found that, with all the dust flying about, I could see nothing through my periscope. I had a signaller with me, so informed brigade headquarters that I was going to leave the dugout and would lie outside. Communication was more difficult there, but at least I could see something. Unfortunately, my first view was not very encouraging. The two tanks were coming down the hillside behind, towards Mouquet Farm. The first went into a large shell hole on our side of the farm and remained stuck there. Very soon the second did likewise. Neither was able to neutralise the Germans in the farm who continued to shoot into the backs of our troops advancing up the hill.

From the slopes above Fricourt

old no mans land

Contalmaison
Chateau

Fricourt wood

mametz wood

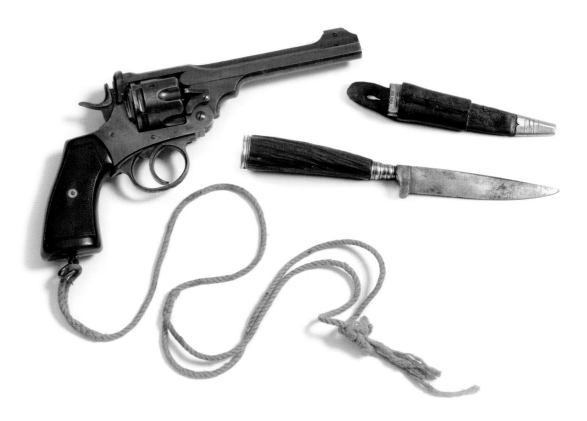

Despite these setbacks, Mouquet Farm was successfully captured by the British infantry that evening, following hand-to-hand fighting among the rubble. Tanks were utilised in the battle but, as with the assault on Morval, they proved more useful in a supporting role rather than when leading the attack. Although both tanks struggled to reach the farm, their crews were still able to use their machine guns and at 5.30pm, following smoke bombs fired into the rubble, the survivors of the German garrison surrendered.

Opposite Muirhead Bone, *An Artillery Barrage on the Somme Battlefield: Mametz Wood, Contalmaison Château, Fricourt Wood and Delville Wood in the distance. Drawn from King's Hill, Fricourt, September, 1916*, 1916. **Art.IWM ART 2098**

Above left The Webley Mark V revolver was the standard British service revolver at the outbreak of the First World War. This particular example was the property of 2nd Lieutenant J R R Tolkien – later to gain fame as author of *The Hobbit* and *The Lord of the Rings*, in addition to enjoying a distinguished academic career. Tolkein joined the 11th Battalion Lancashire Fusiliers in France in June 1916, shortly before the Somme, and during the battle served as the battalion signals officer. In late October 1916 he contracted trench fever and was sent back to England in early November, spending much of the rest of the war convalescing. It was at this time that he began to write early versions of his 'Middle Earth' stories. **FIR 11492**

Above right War trophies were popular souvenirs among the troops, especially to send home to impress family and friends. This German hunting knife, brought to the front for use as a trench dagger, was captured from a soldier of the 109th Pioneers at Mametz on 1 September 1916 by Machine Gun Corps officer Lieutenant J Best. Best was promoted to the rank of Major shortly before his death at Amiens in May 1918. **WEA 835.1**

Meanwhile, further to the left of the line, the attack on Thiepval began well. The attackers managed to stay ahead of the German artillery fire while, as was the case at Mouquet Farm, fighting began at close quarters within the ruins of the village. The German defenders refused to give up their position and in many cases fought to the death, but by the end of the day the village was in British hands. The key role in the assault had been played by the infantry of General Sir Ivor Maxse's 18th Division, whose considerable training and preparation before the battle was reflected in their success. With Thiepval now captured, the assault on the Schwaben Redoubt could begin the following day, with the task allotted to 53rd Brigade.

Thiepval and the Schwaben Redoubt were connected by a series of formidable fortifications and trenches, which included Stuff Redoubt and Zollern Redoubt. Central to these defensive works was Regina Trench. Partially captured by the Canadians on 1 October, and attacked by them again a week later, Regina was mostly taken on 21 October by the 4th Canadian Division and two British divisions, the 18th and 25th. The tough fighting at close quarters was recalled by Private Reginald Emmett of the 11th Battalion Royal Fusiliers, who was allotted the task of 'mopping up' the German dugouts around Thiepval:

I started by shouting down, telling any Germans left to come up. If there was no response I fired a few shots and then threw a bomb down. We got quite a few — some came up holding their hands up and shouting, 'Kamerad!'; others held up photographs of their wives and children. We had to be very quick on them, for some still had a bit of fight left in them and pulled out revolvers, but we soon knocked them off. The survivors were sent back down the line in charge of a corporal, but many got shot on the way, for many of our boys were mad with what they had gone through and the strain of it all, and just shot anything in a German uniform.

Once again, the German skill in building strong defensive works meant that fighting would continue in the area until the following month. Among the British troops involved in the fighting for the Schwaben Redoubt was the 11th Battalion Lancashire Fusiliers signalling officer, John Tolkein, who passed messages back to headquarters from his position in Zollern Trench. Earlier in October, Tolkein had been based for a week in dugouts close to Mouquet Farm and so was very familiar with the Thiepval sector. Some years later he would remember this experience of battle when writing his famous series of books set in the mythical Middle Earth.

Meanwhile, skirmishes continued around the Schwaben Redoubt, which remained a fiercely contested part of the line. Lieutenant Tom Adlam, of the 7th Battalion Bedfordshire and Hertfordshire Regiment, recalled the close-quarter nature of the conflict:

By the time we got this close to the Schwaben Redoubt there was a huge shell crater, a mine crater I think, because it was about 50 feet across. It was all lined with Germans popping away at us. So I got hold of the old bombs again and started trying to bomb them out. After a bit we got them out of there and started charging up the trench, all my men coming on behind very gallantly. We got right to within striking distance of the Schwaben Redoubt itself. Just at that minute I got a bang in the arm and found I was bleeding. So being a bombing officer who could throw with both arms, I used my left arm for a while and I found I could bomb pretty well with it as I could my right. We went on for some time, holding on to this position and working our way up the trenches as far as we could. The men sort of lose all control. There was a German soldier, he'd been wounded, he was in a bad way. He was just moaning, 'Mercy, kamerad, mercy, kamerad'. And this fellow in front of me, one of the nicest men I had in my platoon, he said, 'Mercy you bloody German, take that!' He pointed point-blank at him, just in front of me, but he jerked and missed him. I gave him a shove from behind and said, 'Go on, he won't do any harm. Let's go and get a good one!' It was so funny, the fellow said to me afterwards, 'Sir, I'm glad I missed him!' It was just the heat of the moment you see. Then my C.O. came up and said, 'You're hurt, Tom', I said, 'Only a snick in the arm!' He said, 'Let's have a look at it' and he put a field dressing on it. He said, 'You go on back, you've done enough'.

Above Wooden sign from a reserve trench which ran through the village of Thiepval during the Battle of the Somme. It was named after Lieutenant Colonel Frank Maxwell VC, commander of the 12th Battalion Middlesex Regiment, who led the capture of the chateau at Thiepval in September 1916. **FEQ 25**

Below Lieutenant General's shoulder strap, belonging to the German Commander of Thiepval Garrison. The officer was captured along with 15 other officers and 1,500 prisoners at Les Meules, then sent to II Corps Headquarters where he gave this shoulder strap to Lieutenant M E Rowland of the Royal Engineers as a war souvenir. **INS 7583**

Flag made in the field and flown at the headquarters of 100th Machine Gun Company at High Wood, Delville Wood, Les Boeufs and Le Transloy. The flag belonged to Lieutenant Colonel Graham Seton Hutchison, the 100th Brigade Machine Gun Commander. **FLA 967**

A horse-drawn limber takes ammunition to the forward guns along the Lesboeufs Road, outside Flers, in November 1916 during the final stages of the Somme offensive. The horses are up to their knees in liquid mud, with the ground having now become a quagmire. **Q 2980**

Numerous attacks and counter-attacks meant that only the southern and eastern areas of the Redoubt remained in British hands for much of the battle, until the Germans were finally ousted on 14 October. This marked the end of the Battle of Thiepval Ridge which, while being claimed as a success by the British and French, had really only served to reveal that the German defences remained remarkably strong. There was little indication that their reserves were nearing exhaustion, and the battle of attrition therefore continued with no immediate resolution in sight.

With winter fast approaching and, with it, the poor weather conditions which would make any continued offensive almost impossible to fight, Haig had only a limited opportunity to continue the Somme campaign. Following the capture of Thiepval, he initially intended to involve the Third, Fourth and Reserve Armies in a combined offensive, spread over a wide front – in effect, throwing everything he had at the Germans. However, the onset of bad weather prevented these plans from coming to fruition and instead a series of smaller offensives was arranged. The Fourth Army was tasked with what would become known as the Battles of the Transloy Ridges to the right of the line, and the Reserve Army was to lead the Battle of the Ancre to the left. This fighting was undertaken in terrible conditions, as Captain Alfred Bundy recorded in his diary for the end of October 1916:

During the Battle of the Ancre in November 1916, members of a working party, clad in waterproof capes and thigh-length wader boots, await orders in the rain at St Pierre Divion. While the Battle of the Somme began with fine summer weather in July, by this point in the late autumn the weather had deteriorated markedly, and the increasingly wet and muddy conditions were a contributing factor in calling an end to the campaign. **Q 4602**

Liquid mud lies at the bottom, in some places two feet deep. Several times this filthy slime has been well above my field boots and my legs and feet are, and have been for hours, completely wet and numbed with cold. In my own misery I feel intensely for the men who, with puttees only, are worse off than the officers. They are marvellous in their uncomplaining fortitude but I think I understand the secret. Contrary to what one might believe to be the case, I have found that the desire to live is strongest when the conditions of existence are most dangerous and depressing. It is hope for an escape to the normal and safe that keeps the spirits up. I do not, and will not now, believe that it is natural to long for death in conditions of the most abject temporary misery – the more the misery, the greater the desire to live.

A key role in the Transloy battles would be played by the Canadian, Australian and New Zealand troops. Between 1 and 20 October, on the battle's extreme right, the Fourth Army staggered slowly but surely towards Le Transloy, with the 23rd Division capturing Le Sars on the Albert–Bapaume road on 7 October. Major Harry Dillon was in command of the 1st Battalion West Yorkshire Regiment, who were involved in one of the many attacks made towards Le Transloy. More often than not, these attacks were far from successful:

We have been brought back about three miles. This last battle was so horrible and so terrific that I shall not try to describe it to you. We did part of what we were asked to do but could do no more for the simple reason that there was nobody left to do it, and the few survivors were too shaken and dazed to do any more attacking, our trenches were just heaps of bloody earth. My General just sent me a line and says, 'Your battalion had a most exasperating time up in the line. Great credit is due to you all for carrying on so well under such disadvantageous circumstances.' We are in reserve now and I have had a big reinforcement last night, so perhaps they will send us in again. They are at it hammer and tongs and we are just waiting in case we are wanted. This battle seems to go on with ever increasing fury. An endless procession of more and more men and guns. The men are absolutely splendid and nobody seems to take any account of life whatever. Well if I live through this battle I think I shall have seen war at its worst. Hell must have some bottom.

Below A wounded British soldier at a dressing station in Aveluy Wood shows a comrade his damaged steel helmet, which has had a piece blown out of it. This photograph was taken on 13 November 1916, the opening day of the British attack astride the Ancre. **Q 4510**

Opposite British troops receiving hot food from field kitchens in the Ancre sector, during October 1916. Hot food was not generally supplied to front line soldiers until late 1915 and, even after this date, it was by no means a regular occurrence. **Q 1582**

The Reverend David Railton was an Anglican Chaplain attached to the 19th Battalion London Regiment, and his duties of administering to the wounded and dying meant that he witnessed much of the suffering resulting from the attempts to take the Transloy Ridge. Horses were used extensively for transport throughout the fighting on the Western Front, and many animals became casualties:

> This morning at 12.30 to 1.00am I was coming back from a dressing station and I came through the transport lines. I had a flash light and I turned it on some of the dear horses and patted them. I went on to the next. The light showed a great hole all stopped up with wadding... I went on and the next one had a hole in the head, the next in the legs and body, and so it went on. The flash light showed up enough to tell me how terribly they had been wounded in taking food up to our men. But all was silent. Only one was breathing a little heavily, that was all. I had just come from a dressing station. Our men suffer very bravely. But if you went into a dressing station after a battle blindfolded you would know at once from occasional groans and expressions and movements that men were there in pain. If you went through our transport lines blindfolded you would not have known that seven of our horses were wounded, for they suffer in absolute silence.

By now, the constant rain had turned the battleground into a boggy quagmire. Immediately ahead, lying between Le Sars and Bapaume, was the Butte de Warlencourt, a strongly defended German position based above an ancient burial mound. Here the attackers were thwarted by numerous German machine gun nests that caused significant casualties, especially among the South African troops. The

60-foot high chalk mound dominated the landscape, and its capture would provide a strategically important outpost, overlooking the German-held town of Bapaume. The Fourth Army renewed their attack on 23 October but, by the time of the final attempt on 5 November, they had achieved little result and Transloy and the Butte were still in German hands. It would not be until February the following year that the Butte was finally captured by the 2nd Australian Division, following the general retreat of the German Army towards the Hindenburg Line.

As far as the Battle of the Somme was concerned, the end was now in sight. Autumn was fast turning into winter and the weather had deteriorated markedly, causing poor visibility for aerial observation and constant mud for the ground troops to trudge through. While the French Sixth Army launched an offensive at St Pierre Vaast Wood on 7 November, the last real act of the Somme offensive took place north of Thiepval, in the sector around the River Ancre, between 13 and 19 November. The Battle of the Ancre was planned in a rather half-hearted manner, however, and had been subject to repeated postponements. It was hoped that a late British success might create a favourable impression at the inter-Allied conference being held at Chantilly on 15 November.

In dreadful conditions, the Fifth Army, as Gough's Reserve Army had by now been renamed, attacked astride the River Ancre with the aim of reducing the German salient between Serre and the Albert–Bapaume road. Their objectives, which included the villages of Serre, Beaucourt and Beaumont Hamel, together with Redan Ridge, were all originally objectives assigned to the very first act of the Somme offensive on 1 July. Many of the troops involved would have been aware of this, and one can imagine the weary resignation as they prepared to fight for the same ground. Joe Murray of the Hood Battalion, 63rd (Royal Naval) Division, recalled the nervous anticipation of waiting in the early morning of Monday 13 November until Zero Hour, when he and his men would go over the top into battle:

German barbed wire entanglement at Beaucourt, east of Beaumont Hamel, during the Battle of the Ancre in November 1916. The village was captured on 14 November by the 63rd (Royal Naval) Division during the closing phase of the Battle of the Somme. Obstacles such as this were common elements of trench construction throughout the First World War, and were clear reasons why armoured vehicles such as tanks were required in order to assist in breaking through the enemy's defences. Q 4593

In the early hours of the morning, round about five o'clock, we were all woken, perishing cold. About 05.30, most of us started getting warmed up a bit, dancing about, quietly. Then we had to fix bayonets. There's always a noise with fixing bayonets, a clink, a metallic noise, so you put your tunic round it to deaden it. At 5.45, all of a sudden, behind us, the whole sky was red, it reminded me of home a couple of miles across the valley from Consett Iron Company, when they used to draw the furnaces there. Immediately afterwards you could hear the shells going over your head and you could almost feel the shells. Then we heard the sound, the light was first, the shell was next and then the sound. There was a lot of them falling short. But at the same time, you know, were it not for the artillery barrage then we'd all have been slaughtered – we wouldn't have advanced at all. So it was the lesser of the two evils. We knew we had seven or eight minutes, then the Germans would retaliate, they would bombard beyond the front line to the reserves coming up – which we knew would be there. So the quicker we got out of our positions towards the barrage, the safer we were.

Gough's force began their attack through natural dense fog, which fortuitously acted as an effective cover. The Royal Naval Division successfully captured Beaucourt, yet Redan Ridge and the village of Serre remained in German hands. The 51st (Highland) Division took Beaumont Hamel, following the detonation of a new 30,000 lb mine dug beneath the old Hawthorn Ridge crater (which doubled the size of the resulting hole and eliminated a large number of German defenders in the process). As Private Arthur Wrench of the 1/4th Battalion Seaforth Highlanders would recall in his diary, any success had been achieved at the usual cost:

Monday 13. Gosh, what a day... The attack began at six. Shortly after, the 5th Seaforths took the third line and with the 8th Argylls got 120 prisoners. They are poor, miserable, dejected-looking creatures and appeared to be either older men or boys and not the usual sort of German soldier. It is really pitiful to see them, they are as scared looking as can be, and ragged. The 51st took over a thousand prisoners, the fog covering the attack in which the Huns were absolutely surprised, many of them still being in bed at the time. I suppose they must have been following their usual custom of getting well down to it every morning when our bombardment started, and so did not expect this attack this morning. Good job for us, for this fact alone has decided the fate of Beaumont Hamel. So the capture was comparatively easy with few casualties, until Fritz realised what was happening, and then the struggle began. They opened fire on all the roads through here to the front so that reinforcements would be cut off.

Tuesday 14. Advance continued well with a fierce barrage again in the morning and stubborn resistance now from the enemy, for he has his guns trained on Beaumont Hamel and his reserves up in action. The battle is terrible and we orderlies have been under orders to stand to for reinforcements if required... It has been a most trying time and a wretched fatiguing day with an extra journey up to Auchonvillers grenade dump at night. Getting up along that road is an ordeal one is not likely to forget in a hurry, and the whole way is congested with guns, transports and ammunition limbers moving forward to new positions. The fog is still thick too, so that the whole column is like a phantom procession emerging into distinct forms and then disappearing again ahead. What a queer unholy feeling it gives you.

During the Battle of the Ancre, the final phase of the Somme offensive, the 51st Division captured over 2,000 prisoners but in return had lost some 2,500 soldiers killed, wounded or missing. This number equated to almost half of the total number of troops who had been involved in the attack.

On Sunday 19 November, the Battle of the Somme officially came to an end. The German tactical position was certainly beginning to deteriorate, but the oncoming winter meant that the British and French were in no position to be able to exploit this to any advantage. During the 142 days since 1 July 1916, the British had seized a strip of territory some 6 miles deep by 20 miles long, yet they were still 3 miles from the German-held town of Bapaume, and the French, further south, had stopped short of capturing Péronne. It had been the greatest battle of the war so far, with the consequent loss of life truly shattering in scale. The immediate offensive was over, yet the First World War would continue for another two years. The Somme itself would be remembered with notoriety not only as a key battle during the immediate conflict, but as one of the most important encounters in the history of modern warfare. Its legacy would be a far-reaching and long-lasting one.

Our dugout
command front
1917

ART AND THE SOMME

Richard Slocombe

Britain's first experience of mass mobilisation in 1914 drew men into the ranks of the British Army from all backgrounds and professions. Artists and illustrators were no exception, and enlisted in the same patriotic spirit and sense of collective duty. For many of these 'soldier-artists' the first taste of combat would be in the crucible of the Somme offensive in 1916. The battle, be it costly catastrophe or Pyrrhic victory, remains central to the British understanding of the First World War. Yet its visual representation by those who experienced the fighting or its aftermath could be surprising, and reveal unfamiliar aspects of the campaign.

The Somme offensive also created some unlikely soldiers, none more so than 2nd Lieutenant Ernest Howard Shepard, second-in-command of a battery of heavy howitzers. He would become better known as the artist behind the enduringly popular illustrations for *Winnie-the-Pooh* and *The Wind in the Willows*. As a married man with children, Shepard had been under no pressure to enlist at the outset of war but, by early 1915, patriotism encouraged him to indulge a fascination with soldiering. Commissioned in December 1915, he joined the 105th Siege Battery, Royal Garrison Artillery a month later. They arrived on the Somme in July 1916, taking up positions near Bronfay Farm. Shepard wrote home almost daily, and with sketchbook close-to-hand made several drawings of his surroundings. *Our BC Post, Copse B, near Maricourt, Somme, August 1916* (opposite) was one such, a delicate pencil and wash drawing capturing the basic but orderly conditions of Shepard's command post. This and the sunlight flooding into the dugout conveyed an ordered calm, and offered no hint of the brutal business in which Shepard was engaged.

Back in London Shepard's wartime duties were not assumed particularly onerous, for he was still expected to deliver cartoons for *Punch* and other titles. These stoically mocked the routines and rigours of trench life. Yet as Shepard moved from the Somme to other sectors of the Western Front, his private impressions of the front revealed an altogether more sensitive response to war.

Like Shepard, the war intervened mid-career for the St Ives painter, Borlase Smart. Joining the Cornish art colony in 1913, he was mentored by the Anglo–Swedish painter Julius Olsson, an artist famed for his moonlit seascapes and rich bravura style. Smart acquired a similarly lush Impressionist technique, sharing also Olsson's interest in oceanic light and taste for drama.

Opposite E H Shepard, *Our BC Post, Copse B, near Maricourt, Somme, August 1916*, 1916. **Art.IWM ART 5911**

R Borlase Smart, *Ruins near the Somme*, 1917. **Art.IWM ART 4476**

Smart enlisted immediately on the outbreak of war, was gazetted the following year to the 2/24th Battalion London Regiment (The Queens), and was sent to the Somme in July 1916. It was a brief posting, for Smart was recalled in September to join the Machine Gun Corps. Even so, the experience of the frontline had made its impact and he produced almost 40 war drawings in charcoal and wash, 13 of which featured the devastated flashpoints of the Somme campaign. Here Smart applied the lessons of Olsson, combining vigorous economy of line with clever use of coloured grounds to invest the best examples with subtle luminosity and melancholic grandeur.

The brevity of Smart's time at the front meant his art was produced from memory and aided by photographs. Smart's drawing of the bombarded village of Fricourt, for example, was derived from Ernest Brooks's official photograph of the village from July 1916. On the other

hand, *A Dug-out* forwent topographical reference, expressing greater interest in the construction of an abandoned German shelter. The inclusion of a smouldering unnamed village in the background was probably an embellishment to add drama to the scene.

Seeking to capitalise on public interest in art by serving soldiers, Smart staged a successful exhibition in July 1917 at the Fine Art Society in London, with the newly formed Imperial War Museum purchasing seven drawings. In light of this, he made an unsuccessful application to become an official war artist for the museum. This was the tail-end of a pioneering scheme formed initially by Britain's propaganda agency, Wellington House, in 1916. The scheme's founding had been almost accidental, arising from a chance meeting between the publisher A P Watt and Muirhead Bone in May 1916. Bone was a widely admired Scottish etcher, who had gained his reputation through meticulously observed industrial and architectural subjects. However, at the age of 40, he was about to receive his conscription papers. Watt reported his encounter to Wellington House, arguing that Bone would be, as he put it, 'wasted as canon-fodder'. It happened that the propaganda agency had a role for the Glaswegian printmaker, as a dearth in the variety of photographic material necessitated the employment of an artist to supplement Wellington House journals with images of the front. Although Bone had no experience of black and white illustration, he was renowned for his ability to work rapidly outdoors. Thus, on 16 August 1916 Bone was sent to France at the height of the Somme offensive, as an honorary 2nd Lieutenant and Britain's first official war artist.

Below The ruined village of Fricourt, July 1916. **121. Q 854**

Bottom R Borlase Smart, *Fricourt,* 1917. **Art. IWM ART 4471**

Touring the battlefields in the south – Maricourt, Fricourt, Mametz Wood, High Wood, Delville Wood and Pozières – Bone worked quickly in pencil, pen, charcoal and chalk, and by 6 October had completed approximately 150 finished drawings. Impressed, Wellington House offered Bone his own publication, *The Western Front.* Comprising ten monthly instalments it aimed to exploit Bone's international repute (he was popular even in Germany) to generate an authoritative, measured and enduring version of events – or, as the critic Charles Marriott fulsomely wrote in *Country Life* (30 December 1916): 'the form and quality belong to the permanent record, to be bound and treasured as a superb pictorial history of the war on its Western Front by one of the greatest artists living'. True enough, works such as *An Artillery Barrage on the Somme Battlefield,* with its sketchy, on-the-spot vitality, had all the look of impartial records. It is only in Bone's drawing of Britain's new wonder weapon, the tank, that he allowed himself some dramatic licence, catching it in raking light as it pitched menacingly over a trench.

The plausibility of Bone's vision was critical during his second sojourn to the Somme in May 1917. It coincided with the aftermath of the German Army's scorched-earth policy preceding its withdrawal to the Hindenburg Line. Naturally, the Germans' actions were a gift to Britain's propagandists, and they presented the destruction as a cynical act of vandalism on French rural society and tradition. Bone's drawings of this period were more finished and carefully composed than his earlier work of 1916. Indeed, his drawings of razed chateaux, felled orchards and demolished farmsteads formed a pastiche of topographical landscape tradition, incorporating picturesque elements to heighten a sense of Teutonic invasiveness. Published in an edition of *The Western Front,* propaganda was achieved by a symbiosis of Bone's drawings and text by C E Montague, former lead writer for the *Manchester Guardian.* Montague's text offered a slanted interpretation of seemingly neutral drawings, to which Bone's carefully composed and detailed depictions conferred authority.

Despite considerable investment, *The Western Front* was only a moderate success. The press complained that Bone's drawings were distant and disengaged, and too fixated with war damage. 'Like a peep down the wrong end of a telescope', quipped one newspaper. Perhaps worst of all, *The Western Front* was derided by the soldiers themselves. Wilfred Owen, newly arrived at the

Top Muirhead Bone, *A Street in Contalmaison, August 1916,* 1916.
Art.IWM ART 2049

Above Muirhead Bone, *Haplincourt Chateau, near Brie on the Somme, May 1917,* 1917.
Art.IWM ART 2161

Opposite William Orpen, *The Artist: Self Portrait,* c.1917.
Art.IWM ART 2993

France. For Orpen the war began quietly enough, his society contacts securing him a safe post at the Army Service Corps headquarters in London. However, he grew frustrated by the attention that lesser known artists were gaining for their war art and, learning of Wellington House's employment of artists, drew again on his connections. Usefully, these included the Secretary of State for War, and in April 1917 'Major Orpen' arrived in France as Britain's latest official war artist.

His first destination was the Somme. The campaign had ended five months earlier but the sight of the battlefield made an immediate, indelible impression and elicited ambivalent feelings, later recalled in *An Onlooker in France:* 'I shall never forget my first sight of the Somme battlefields .... Nothing but mud, water, crosses and broken Tanks; miles and miles of it, horrible and terrible, but with a noble dignity of its own.'

Although Orpen experienced an instinctive 'longing to get away', the Somme exercised a powerful hold over him and in August he was back. Based in the Thiepval sector, the artist found the battlefield much-changed, but no less affecting: 'The dreary dismal mud was baked white and pure — dazzling white. White daisies, red poppies and a blue flower, great masses of them, stretched for miles and miles. The sky was a pure dark blue, and the whole air ... thick with white butterflies. It was like an enchanted land; but in place of fairies there were thousands of white crosses, marked *Unknown British Soldier.*'

Despite the profusion of nature, Orpen found the area disorientating and unnerving. The occupying British forces may have buried their dead, but they left the Germans to rot where they lay. Planting his easel amid the detritus, and abandoning his usual earthy hues for a brilliant Post-Impressionist palette, Orpen produced over 20 canvases epitomising the macabre oddity of the location. *Thiepval* (1917), for example (page 163), captures a grisly encounter with 'the remains of a Britisher and a Bosche — just skulls, bones, garments.' In *Dead Germans in a Trench* (1917) (page 186) the chalky Picardy soil and deep blue sky typically combine to provide a 'queer fantastic' setting for two putrefying German corpses. Likewise, *A Gunner's Shelter in a Trench, Thiepval* (1917) (page 14) finds Orpen again in the labyrinth of trenches; an eerie, perhaps portentous, calm having descended, with him alone amid the lengthening shadows and discarded effects of former occupants.

front in late 1916, was aggrieved at Montague's attempts, as he saw it, to sanitise the frontlines with comparisons with the English countryside. 'Those "Somme pictures"', he said, 'are the laughing stock of the army'. He went on: 'No man's land under snow is like the face of the moon, chaotic, crater ridden, uninhabitable, awful, the abode of madness. To call it England!'

It was another artist who most dramatically captured the natural and human desolation of the Somme — William Orpen. By virtue of his prodigious talent, the Dubliner had risen to become England's leading society portraitist, but in wartime embarked upon a remarkable artistic and spiritual journey into the darker recesses of the human psyche. It yielded some of the most arresting Somme images and a candid wartime memoir, *An Onlooker in*

When exhibited in May 1918, these paintings disturbed even critics accustomed to images of war. An article in *The Times*, 'Art At The Front', dated 25 May 1918, commented: 'Mr Orpen is certainly not a sentimentalist; he seems to paint [the corpses] with cold, serene skill, just as he might paint a bunch of flowers.' The paintings would themselves become the backdrop to stranger images, ones that seemed less the product of dispassionate observation and more the expression of fevered imagination. *A Gunner's Shelter* thus becomes the setting for Orpen's gruesome *A Dead German in a Trench* (1917) (page 60). The subject, just skeletal remains partially obscured by a great coat, seems to spew forth from a poisoned earth amid a dreamlike netherworld manifested in ghostly negative.

Even with Orpen's presence, Wellington House's demands on Muirhead Bone pushed him to exhaustion. This and his work's lukewarm reception forced his employers to expand and diversify its pool of artists in 1917. Notably, following the success of exhibitions by young 'soldier-artists' such as C R W Nevinson and Paul Nash, there was an increasing focus on youth. The avuncular Bone was a willing champion, and proved instrumental in securing official commissions for Nevinson and Nash in 1917. They were joined in the summer of 1918 by a 24 year-old modernist and artilleryman, William Roberts.

Roberts had been, in 1914, the youngest follower of Vorticism, led by the mercurial Wyndham Lewis. The Vorticists plundered elements of Cubism and Italian Futurism to devise an art for a new iconoclastic Anglo-Saxon society committed to aggressive industrialism and urbanisation. Consequently, Roberts and Lewis were less interested in war when it broke out and more so in their developing art, which by 1915 approached pure abstraction. That same year Vorticist aspirations were halted when its male adherents, having 'attested' under the Lord Derby Scheme, were called up for duty. Roberts eventually joined the Royal Field Artillery in France in August 1916.

Soldiering is seldom conducive to art, and serving 'soldier-artists' who produced any work of note usually did so when on leave or were reliant on the favour of sympathetic commanding officers – but not so Roberts. His opportunities to capture his experiences in art were initially limited and sometimes hampered by his superiors, but his fortunes changed significantly when he was accepted for official employment with the Canadian War Memorials Fund in 1918. The scheme, devised by the Canadian tycoon Max Aitken, Lord Beaverbrook, sought a series of large-scale canvases encompassing his country's contribution to the war. Founded in November 1916 it drew both Canadian and British artists, including Roberts's Vorticist cohort Lewis. Despite his presence and that of other key British modernists, artists were instructed to constrain experimental tendencies and undertake subjects selected for them. Even so, Roberts's *The First German Gas Attack at Ypres* (1918) was a magisterial painting that captured the moment when the choking, panic-stricken French colonial 'Zouaves' careered into their own lines.

Beaverbrook's subsequent appointment as British Minister of Information in March 1918 yielded more work for Roberts, facilitating the formation of the British War Memorials Committee (BWMC) along similar lines as the Canadian scheme. Under the novelist Arnold Bennett, the new scheme allowed greater freedom in style and selection of subjects. Roberts was encouraged to produce a large canvas of 'an active service scene [which in its] execution would draw upon his own experiences'. He was required to submit alongside his memorial painting all work produced during his commission, including preparatory drawings. These provide an intriguing insight into Roberts' stylistic development over the latter part of the war – ranging from geometrically abstract forms to an evolving stylised figuration that later defined his post-war output. They also show Roberts considering a number of subjects for his memorial canvas, including an interpretation of the Battle of Delville Wood. Roberts of course had not seen the fighting, and his pencil and red chalk drawing was a deviation from the BWMC's terms of reference. Like *The First German Gas Attack* its horizon is obscured, flattening the picture plane. This was further emphasised by the simple geometric forms of the drawing's elements, combining to generate a schematic whole. Nevertheless, the jagged angularity of the charging figures and cratered landscape succeed in conveying the base energy and confusion of battle, and provide an intriguing glimpse at the potential of Cubist aesthetics when applied to history painting. The choice of subject may have been a response to the recollections of Delville Wood by longer serving members of Roberts's unit. If realised as a memorial canvas it would have been one of the few BWMC commissions to feature combat. In the event Roberts, perhaps not risking a return to a volatile Western Front in autumn 1918, opted for the more mundane subject of a shell dump near Reading.

The action at Delville Wood was eventually officially commemorated in 1924. Alfred Turner's bronze *Castor and Pollux*, of which IWM holds a maquette (page 200), dominated the South African National Memorial at Longueval. The piece was characteristic of the post-war resurgence of naturalism in British sculpture, and

a reliance on classical hyperbole to conceptualise the enormity of the conflict's sacrifice. Castor and Pollux, the twins of Greco—Roman mythology, represented a South African union of British colonists and Boer settlers answering the call of the mother country. The prevalence of this approach was due in no small part to Sir George Frampton, a sculptor now remembered for his Peter Pan statue in London's Kensington Gardens, but who from 1919 was the Royal Academy's chief spokesman on war memorials. Frampton believed that, when remembering the war dead, 'finer results are generally obtained by the use of symbolic figures... For it is difficult to make a portrait more than a type, whereas an allegorical group may embody a whole idea'.

Below Paul Nash, *The Ypres Salient at Night,* 1918. **Art.IWM ART 1145**   *Opposite* C R W Nevinson, *A Group of Soldiers,* 1917. **Art.IWM ART 520**

Alfred Turner, like Frampton, was an adherent of 'New Sculpture'. Arising in late Victorian England, and drawing inspiration from the French naturalist sculptor, Jules Dalou, the movement was characterised by its fine modelling and aestheticisation of the human figure. However, it was its practitioners' attempts to invest traditional classical subjects with modern psychological insight that set New Sculpture apart, the best examples of which possess a brooding introspection. It was unsurprising that Frampton considered it the ideal idiom for the war memorials that appeared in Britain and the military cemeteries of northern France from the early 1920s. Melancholic and contemplative these monuments may have been, but their abstraction and mannered sentiment offered little hint of the horror and ferocity of the events that necessitated them. Rather, it emphasised the distance from the battlefield by those who Frampton oxymoronically termed as 'us older men who have won the war over our own firesides'.

Nevertheless, Turner's memorial concluded the many forms of art in which the Somme offensive was visualised. Incorporating every artistic idiom practiced in Britain at the time – Impressionism, Post-Impressionism, Vorticism and the naturalism of New Sculpture – they attest to the vast reach and impact on those who experienced, witnessed and heard about this defining battle of the First World War.

Opposite William Roberts, *An Attack – The Capture of Delville Wood, 1916,* 1918. **Art.IWM ART 1887**

Ministry of Information.

The Capture of Delville Wood.

CHAPTER EIGHT

THE LEGACY OF THE SOMME

Two Australian soldiers inspect the graves in Dartmoor Cemetery, between Albert and Bécordel-Bécourt, in the winter of 1916– 17. The graves in the photograph include those of Private Keith John Wade (7th Australian Field Ambulance, killed on 16 November 1916) and 2nd Lieutenant John Scott Huxley (100th Company Machine Gun Corps, killed on 15 July 1916). The cemetery passed into German hands in March 1918, but was retaken five months later by the 12th Division. While Private Wade's grave remains intact, 2nd Lieutenant Huxley now has no known grave and is commemorated on the Thiepval Memorial. **E(AUS) 166**

The cost in lives due to the Battle of the Somme was enormous. While 1 July 1916 has gone down in history as the worst day for the British Army in terms of the casualty figures sustained and the limited objectives achieved, the on-going battle throughout the subsequent five months should not be forgotten. During the entire campaign, the casualty figures were staggering. The estimates for German casualties on the Somme vary, but between 500,000 and 600,000 soldiers were killed, missing or captured. The French suffered 204,253 total casualties, and the British 419,654. Of this number, some 127,751 British soldiers died between 1 July and 20 November 1916, at an average of 893 per day. With a large proportion of those troops involved in the battle having enlisted into the Pals Battalions of Kitchener's New Army, towns like Sheffield were badly hit by casualties, as a schoolgirl from the time recalled:

> There were sheets and sheets in the paper of the dead and wounded with photographs, where they could get them, of the men. Of course everybody rushed to the paper every day to see if there was anyone they knew. When we got to know of anybody at the school, the headmaster announced them if they had been old boys. I was brought out of class to be told that my cousin had been killed. There were numerous services in churches. It was a very, very sad time – practically everybody was in mourning. People were in deep black, the men if they couldn't wear black wore black armbands as a mark of respect. The city was really shrouded in gloom. They were very, very sad and nothing seemed to matter anymore.

A service at a street shrine located outside a church in Acton Lane, west London. Street shrines became an increasingly common expression of remembrance for the dead, particularly in working-class areas, as the casualty list lengthened during and after the Battle of the Somme. With many of the Pals Battalions suffering high casualties, whole communities were affected by the war in a way which had rarely been experienced by those on the home front before. **HU 58985**

The skeleton of a German soldier lying outside a dugout at Beaumont Hamel. The total British, French and German casualties throughout the Battle of the Somme were in the region of 1,200,000 killed, wounded or captured. This photograph was memorably featured in the famous title sequence to the BBC's ground-breaking documentary series *The Great War*, first shown in 1964. **Q 2041**

However, despite the fact that over the last century the Battle of the Somme has been regarded by many in Britain and her former Empire as symbolic of the slaughter of the First World War, with the first day in particular seen as a terrible highpoint for casualties, the French had endured far worse. On 22 August 1914, for instance, they had suffered 27,000 killed in a single day, while the ongoing war of attrition at Verdun had created their own national synonym for bloodshed and sacrifice. The German Army suffered the greatest number of casualties, perhaps reflecting the determination shown by the defenders in holding their positions in the face of such an onslaught. While not disparaging the incredible sacrifice made by British lives and the Somme's continuing role in the collective memory of the nation, the idea that it was an exclusively British battle could not be further from the truth.

Personal accounts written during the battle, such as the following diary entry by Arthur Wrench recording the events of 16 November during the Battle of the Ancre, suggest that in many cases the Somme had led soldiers to question their own involvement. With so many deaths and the possibility of one's body not even receiving a basic burial, the battle called into debate each soldier's reasons for fighting:

> Fritz has made it one of the most awful days imaginable for us, and up that valley is a terror of a place. The Seaforth Headquarters are situated on sloping ground directly facing the line, being German dugouts, and also overlook a German cemetery. A veranda runs around the dugouts too and it was smashed now when one of the dugouts was blown in today during a strafe when 500 5.9 shells were hurled about the place. This was just in one strafe too, and in the cemetery not one single cross is left standing over a German soldier's grave, but some of the bodies there are torn up again and lie scattered all over the place. It is horrible to see. Perhaps the Germans are not even human to violate the last resting place of their own men who have given their lives for their country, and it strikes me there is not much glory these days in dying for your country. A whole platoon of Seaforths was wiped out there too.

The clear result of these high casualty figures is that the Battle of the Somme is still frequently perceived through the prism of the first day, in which so many died for little gain, with the battle as a whole often regarded as nothing less than senseless slaughter. Careful consideration of the reasons for which the campaign was fought, the difficulties faced in executing the battle plans, and the inexperience of both troops and commanders in fighting this new industrialised form of warfare are often overlooked in favour of a more simplistic assessment.

Opposite William Orpen, *A Highlander Passing a Grave*, 1917. **Art.IWM ART 2995**

Above German dead in a shell hole located between Carnoy and Montauban, in the southernmost sector of the British Fourth Army's front line. Although the Battle of the Somme was costly for Britain, it was described by a German staff officer as the 'bloody grave of the German field army'. It has been estimated that Germany suffered as many as 600,000 casualties throughout the campaign. **Q 65442**

Opposite Other ranks stand to attention as an officer reads from the Bible at the funeral of an Australian soldier at Becourt Wood, during August 1916. The stretcher lying in the foreground appears to be blood-soaked. Burials and grave markers were often rudimentary until after the war, when the Imperial War Graves Commission worked to amalgamate burial sites and establish proper cemeteries. **Q 905**

The blame for the high casualties has generally fallen on Haig, Rawlinson and the rest of the High Command who, it is argued, insisted blindly on continuing the attack despite the ever-mounting heaps of dead. Even observing the battle as part of a 'learning curve', which the commanders had to accept before changing their tactics, is sometimes seen as insulting to those ordinary men who sacrificed themselves for their leaders to 'learn'. Much of this cultural attitude of blame can be ascribed to books written years after the war. Indeed, the Battle of the Somme was being written about and analysed even while it was still being fought, and to this day the military history section of any bookshop or library can be guaranteed to include books covering the subject.

In the decades following the battle its history was, for much of the time, inextricably linked with the disenchanted literature and poetry generated by a small number of participants. The popular works by authors such as Siegfried Sassoon, Edmund Blunden and Robert Graves were appreciated by many who felt that, while the war may have seemed justified at the time, with hindsight there was a lot to be critical about. This was further muddied by what Professor Peter Simkins has described as the 'stale debate on General-ship', in which the blame for things ranging from high casualty figures to the lack of hot food in the trenches has been directed towards Haig and others. To apportion blame is a very human characteristic.

It is interesting to note that Joan Littlewood's Theatre Workshop play *Oh, What a Lovely War,* first produced in 1963 and followed by a feature film version in 1969, seems to have had a greater effect on British perceptions of the First World War than the following year's 26-part BBC series *The Great War,* which was scripted by the respected historians John Terraine and Correlli Barnett. For more recent generations the BBC's *Blackadder Goes Forth* in 1989 reaffirmed the popular myth of bungling generals and senseless slaughter, and remains the way in which much of the general public still think of the war and the Battle of the Somme in particular. We quickly forget that the world in 1916 was very different to that which we know today. As the historian Peter Hart has argued, 'The fighting was not futile unless the war was futile. The responsibility for all the manifold sacrifices lies not so much with the generals as with the enthusiasm with which the world embraced war in 1914'.

The events of 1916 have now passed from living memory. However, today the battle is studied through the wealth of surviving operational records in The National Archives, supported by personal diaries, letters and eyewitness accounts from archives such as the Imperial War Museum, allowing authors to come up with a more rounded interpretation. Most modern historians would now argue that the Battle of the Somme was both politically and militarily inevitable and, although costly, served to drain the strength from the German Army and by doing so laid the foundations for an ultimate Allied victory. The high casualties sustained throughout the latter half of 1916 were inevitable when fighting the primary enemy on the main field of battle – the Western Front. As Professor Brian Bond has argued, 'The time is surely approaching, if it has not already

arrived, when the First World War can be studied simply as history without polemic, intent or apologies. It has taken a long historical march to reach this vantage point.'

Despite the high cost in casualties, in the longer term the Battle of the Somme can be seen as having been a strategic success. In his despatch of 23 December 1916 – revealingly entitled 'The Opening of the Wearing-Out Battle' – Haig made the observation that:

> The objective of [the] offensive was threefold:
>
> (1) To relieve the pressure on Verdun.
>
> (2) To assist our Allies in the other theatres of the war by stopping any further transfer of German troops from the Western front.
>
> (3) To wear down the strength of the forces opposed to us.
>
> Any one of these results is in itself sufficient to justify the Somme battle. The attainment of all three of them affords ample compensation for the splendid efforts of our troops and for the sacrifices made by ourselves and our Allies. They have brought us a long step forward towards the final victory of the Allied cause.

In many ways the whole point of the battle had been the long-term destruction of the German Army, and short-term gains in terms of ground captured were of less importance when considering this wider strategy. Despite having only been driven back a relatively short distance between July and November 1916, the German Army had taken a significant pounding during the offensive and in February 1917 began to withdraw to the previously prepared Hindenburg Line, a series of strong points designed to withstand further Allied attacks. This retreat served to shorten the length of front to be defended, but indicated very clearly that the Germans were not going to engage in any specific operations to defend the Somme and Ancre sectors from this point on. On 25 February 1917, Lieutenant Robert Blackadder recorded in his diary this unexpected development:

> Great news came in last night – the Germans have retired from our immediate front. The infantry were pushing forward and reconnoitring and officers were detailed from some batteries to go forward and reconnoitre for observation posts on the ridges in front of Puisieux. The Germans have carried this movement out under cover of the thick mist of the last week and it explains their silence yesterday and the presence of the General. During the day we had received instructions not to fire in certain areas – no doubt our patrols were pushing out yesterday.

The following month, Captain Arthur Gibbs of the Welsh Guards could address his letter home as being from Hale, near Péronne, as he revealed that the German decision to retreat had been a considered one:

> The Germans have left any number of booby traps behind, most of them intensely practical. They put a splendid helmet out, for somebody to pick up as a souvenir. Directly you touch it, off it goes, or rather the bomb inside does! You go down into a cellar, put your foot on a step, which sends off a mine. You sit down on a chair, and are blown out of it, sooner than you bargained for. And so on. There was a very frightening affair, just by one of our posts. There was a big barbed-wire barrier across the road, and several electric wires running from it, quite inconspicuously, to half a dozen big shells by the road side. There was a dummy gun, too, by the shells. Naturally, we gave this a wide berth, and scarcely dared breathe when we were near. We got an RE to cut the wires and take the thing to pieces, and the whole thing was a hoax. There was nothing to set off the shells and the wires led to nowhere. How the Boche would have laughed if he could have seen us! In another place we found three empty coffins, labelled 'For Tommy'!

All of the senior Allied commanders on the Somme including Joffre, Haig, Rawlinson and Gough certainly made mistakes in judgement and, while it could be argued that they took their time to correct them, they did learn important lessons which would eventually be put into practice. The troops too learned a lot from the experience of the Somme and, even while the battle raged, tactical improvements were introduced and spread via training programmes. Closer cooperation with the French Army, who had a greater level of experience in battle, had helped a great deal. Infantry were restructured and granted greater freedom on the battlefield in order to facilitate a more mobile style of warfare, allowing troops to change direction during attacks more easily and flow around opposition.

British troops cross the River Somme at Brie, near Péronne, on 20 March 1917. By this time the German Army had withdrawn to strategic points on the Hindenburg Line and the Allies adopted new positions accordingly. **Q 1828**

Following the German offensive at Verdun, the Somme had seized back the initiative for the Allies. The British had emerged as a major player in the land battle, having previously been the junior partner in the Anglo–French alliance. Britain and the troops from her Empire had proved themselves as strong fighters alongside the French, pioneering new weaponry and making great strides in the development of aircraft and tanks in order to fight the war. The British Army evolved throughout the conflict from a small inexperienced expeditionary force, through the addition of a large body of volunteer and conscripted 'amateurs', to a highly professional and effective Army.

Above A railway station and sidings are blown up by the Germans as part of a deliberate programme of destruction during their retreat to the Hindenburg Line in the spring of 1917. This new line of defence would allow them to strengthen their position in readiness for further attacks by the Allies. **Q 57515**

Opposite Dump of bombs and other stores, abandoned after the Germans were driven out of St Pierre-Divion by the 39th Division on 13 November 1916. Among the equipment left behind is a wealth of stick grenades and steel helmets. **Q 4586**

The greatest lessons learned were arguably those involving the new technology of war and how to apply it most appropriately. Artillery was still very much the key to victory, and some success had been achieved through the 'bite and hold' technique of attacking a short length of front line with a quick, hard artillery bombardment, then using a creeping barrage to cover the infantry assault which would consolidate its position. But this relied on a huge number of guns and ammunition, as well as logistical improvements which would not really be in place until nearer the end of the war. Greater experience meant that the gunners could put more accurate range-finding techniques into operation, which was the first step to firing their guns without having to register them beforehand; predicted fire would be an important strategic gain. The introduction of the armoured tank had shown that such vehicles could make a real difference when given a supporting role in infantry attacks, yet the technology in 1916 remained primitive and their potential was still to be fully realised in battle. Aircraft, however, were now seen as a crucial weapon of war, not only in attacking areas of the enemy's ground which could not be reached by normal artillery shells, but in their role as reconnaissance observers, identifying locations for artillery fire and assessing the results of bombardments.

Through this more integrated use of resources and improvements in fighting techniques the Battle of the Somme can be seen as the first stage in the development of the so-called 'All Arms Battle', which would lead the Allies to ultimate victory at the end of 1918. The learning process was a harsh one, as felt by the high casualties sustained throughout the entire war and not only the Somme campaign, but this pain would eventually result in a resolution to the fighting.

The 50th anniversary of the Battle of the Somme fell on 1 July 1966, and many old soldiers took the opportunity to revisit the battlefields, partly to meet with old comrades and reminisce about their good fortune in surviving such a war, but perhaps mainly to pay their respects to the many thousands of soldiers who failed to return from the battle. Among their number was Sidney Appleyard, formerly of the Queen Victoria's Rifles:

The setting sun behind the Commonwealth War Graves Commission Thiepval Memorial, photographed from near Mouquet Farm, 2006.

The War Graves Commission have maintained immaculately the Somme memorial at Thiepval. This is the only place for miles where the flower beds don't have signs telling the public not to walk on them. As one of the war veterans said, 'They would be irrelevant here. I think everyone understands what this earth cost. The only people who really know about it are underneath. I think this anniversary will be the last. When it comes up to 75 years, we'll all be dead too, and the Somme will seem as abstract as Waterloo'.

We know today that this particular war veteran was wrong. Now that we have reached the centennial anniversary of the Somme, the battle has been far from forgotten. New generations have taken on the task of ensuring that the sacrifice of those who lost their lives will always be remembered, while guaranteeing that veterans' recorded experiences of the Somme and the lessons learned from one of the most important battles ever fought will live on for many years to come.

SOURCES

CHAPTER 1
IWM, Private Papers of G K Parker (Documents.11787)
IWM, Interview with Horace Calvert (Sound 9955)
IWM, Private Papers of Captain J I Cohen (Documents.3520)
IWM, Interview with William Underwood (Sound 4247)
IWM, Miscellaneous 955 (Documents.5015)
IWM, Private Papers of Captain J N Pring (Documents.11685)

CHAPTER 2
IWM, Interview with Harold Joseph Hayward (Sound 9422)
IWM, Miscellaneous 3609 (Documents.14044), 'A Munition Girl's Thoughts'.
IWM, Private Papers of W Lafrichoud (Documents.17626)

IN FOCUS: RECRUITING FOR THE SOMME
IWM, Private Papers of R M Luther (Documents.1325)
IWM, Interview with Horace Astin (Sound 11039)
IWM, Private Papers of J H Hird (Documents.14327)
IWM, Private Papers of B L Fensom (Documents.14275)
IWM, Private Papers of J Beeken (Documents.7730)
IWM, Private Papers of G E Dale (Documents.7330)
IWM, Private Papers of R E Foulkes (Documents.2646)
IWM, Private Papers of R J Bailey (Documents.2027)
IWM, Private Papers of Major E I Andrews (Documents.25573)
IWM, Private Papers of T A Jennings (Documents.6596)
IWM, Private Papers of Captain A E Bland (Documents.20673)

CHAPTER 3
IWM, Private Papers of Colonel H E Yeo (Documents.3132)
IWM, Private Papers of W B Stevenson (Documents.4481)
IWM, Private Papers of Lieutenant F L Cassel (Documents.7405)
IWM, Private Papers of Captain H F Bursey (Documents.5646)
IWM, Private Papers of E Blore (Documents.2738)
IWM, Private Papers of Lieutenant Colonel H Wyllie (Documents.3862)
IWM, Private Papers of Captain G McGowan (Documents.18441)
IWM, Interview with George Ashurst (Sound 9875)
IWM, Private Papers of Captain R H V Buxton (Documents.20428)
IWM, Private Papers of Captain D N Meneaud-Lissenburg (Documents.7248)
IWM, Private Papers of 2nd Lieutenant E R Heaton (Documents.12701)

CHAPTER 4
IWM, Private Papers of Lieutenant Colonel W A Vignoles (Documents.6968)
IWM, Private Papers of Major V A H Robeson (Documents.8184), including combat report dated 1 July 1916 by Lieutenant Sidney Cowan
IWM, Private Papers of Brigadier General H C Rees (Documents.7166)
IWM, Interview with Alfred Irwin (Sound 211)
IWM, Private Papers of Captain W T Colyer (Documents.7256)
IWM, Private Papers of Major E I Andrews (Documents.25573)
IWM, Private Papers of Major A E Bundy (Documents.10828)
IWM, Interview with Albert Hurst (Sound 11582)
IWM, Private Papers of Lieutenant F L Cassel (Documents.7405)
IWM, Private Papers of Brigadier G F Ellenberger (Documents.4227)
IWM, Private Papers of Lieutenant E Russell-Jones (Documents.11354)
IWM, Interview with Stewart Jordan (Sound 10391)

IN FOCUS: THE FILM OF THE BATTLE
IWM, Private Papers of F A Robinson (Documents.11335)

CHAPTER 5
IWM, Private Papers of Cyril José (Documents.19925)
IWM, Private Papers of Captain G N Adams (Documents.3497)
IWM, Private Papers of T Phillips (Documents.18022)
IWM, Private Papers of Captain R P Perrin (Documents.25921)
IWM, Private Papers of Major J V Bates (Documents.2854)
IWM, Private Papers of A R Brennan (Documents.12116)
IWM, Private Papers of W & P Robins (Documents.19236)
IWM, Interview with Leonard Ounsworth (Sound 332)
IWM, Private Papers of Colonel G Lillywhite (Documents.7226)
IWM, Private Papers of Wing Commander E J D Routh (Documents.20671)
IWM, Private Papers of O S Blows (Documents.10798)

CHAPTER 6
IWM, Interview with Harold Joseph Hayward (Sound 9422)
IWM, Private Papers of Captain H Horne (Documents.4867)
IWM, Private Papers of Captain D H Pegler (Documents.4357)
IWM, Interview with Stuart H Hastie (Sound 4126)
IWM, Private Papers of Lieutenant E J D Routh (Documents.20671)
IWM, Private Papers of A Russell (Documents.6694)
IWM, Private Papers of Lieutenant Colonel H M Dillon (Documents.4430)

CHAPTER 7

IWM, Private Papers of Captain A Angus (Documents.857)
IWM, Interview with Reginald G Emmett (Sound 16548), typescript account in file.
IWM, Interview with Tom Edwin Adlam (Sound 35)
IWM, Private Papers of Major A E Bundy (Documents.10828)
IWM, Private Papers of Lieutenant Colonel H M Dillon (Documents.4430)
IWM, Private Papers of Reverend D Railton (Documents.4760)
IWM, Interview with Joe Murray (Sound 8201)
IWM, Private Papers of A E Wrench (Documents.3834)

IN FOCUS: ART AND THE SOMME

IWM, War Artists Archive, 140/4 R Borlase Smart
IWM, War Artists Archive, 227/6 William Roberts.

CHAPTER 8

IWM, Interview with Marjorie Llewelyn (Sound 4163)
IWM, Private Papers of A E Wrench (Documents.3834)
IWM, Private Papers of Major R J Blackadder (Documents.927)
IWM, Private Papers of Captain A Gibbs (Documents.12199)
IWM, Private Papers of S W Appleyard (Documents.7990)

PUBLICATIONS

Bloom 2003
Ivo Bloom, *Jean Desmet and the Early Dutch Film Trade*, Amsterdam University Press, 2003

Bond 1991
Professor Brian Bond (ed), *The First World War and British Military History*, Clarendon Press, 1991

Brown 1996
Malcolm Brown, *The Imperial War Museum Book of the Somme*, Sidgwick & Jackson, 1996

Compton 2004
Ann Compton, *The Sculpture of Charles Sargeant Jagger*, Henry Moore Foundation, 2004

Edmonds 1932
Brig-Gen Sir James E Edmonds, *History of the Great War: Military Operations, France and Belgium, 1916*, HMSO, 1932

Fraser, Robertshaw and Roberts 2009
Alastair Fraser, Andrew Robertshaw and Steve Roberts, G*hosts on the Somme: Filming the Battle. June-July 1916*, Pen & Sword, 2009

Hart 2005
Peter Hart, *The Somme*, Weidenfeld & Nicolson, 2005

Hart 2013
Peter Hart, *The Great War*, Profile, 2013

Hynes 1990
Samuel Hynes, *A War Imagined: The First World War and English Culture*, Bodley Head Ltd, 1990

Malins 1920
Geoffrey Malins, *How I Filmed the War*, Herbert Jenkins, 1920 (republished by the Imperial War Museum's Department of Printed Books, 1993, with an introduction by Nicholas Hiley)

Orpen 1924
William Orpen, *An Onlooker in France 1917-1919*, Williams and Norgate, 1924

Prior and Wilson 1992
Robin Prior and Trevor Wilson, *Command on the Western Front*, Blackwell, 1992

Reeves 1999
Nicholas Reeves, *The Power of Film Propaganda: Myth or Reality?* Cassell, 1999

Sheffield and Bourne, 2005
Gary Sheffield and John Bourne (eds), *Douglas Haig: War Diaries and Letters 1914-18*, Weidenfeld & Nicolson, 2005

Simkins 1988
Peter Simkins, Kitchener's Army, T*he Making of the New Armies*, Manchester University Press, 1988

Thompson, 2006
Julian Thompson, *The 1916 Experience: Verdun and the Somme*, Carlton Books, 2006

FILMS

A new digital restoration of the 1916 film *The Battle of the Somme*, with two alternative musical soundtracks and other extras, was released by IWM in 2008, and re-released in 2014:
www.iwmshop.org.uk/product/19580/Battle_of_the_Somme_1916_DVD

IMAGE LIST

All images © IWM unless otherwise stated.

Chapter 1
Q 17486; IWM PST 11639; IWM PST 0409; Q 57167; Q 1384; Art.IWM ART 2963; Q 23659; Q 4032; Q 49217; Q 855; Q 69149

Chapter 2
Q 30018; Q 69626; Art.IWM ART 324; FLA 940; CO 3014; Art. IWM PST 0314; Art. IWM PST 5112; Art.IWM PST 13468; Q 23726; Q 70069; Q 23892

In Focus: Recruiting for the Somme
Art.IWM PST 2734; Art.IWM PST 11910; Q 56658; Art.IWM PST 0318; Q 111825; HU 53725; Q 111826; Art.IWM PST 0332 © Artist's Estate; Q 53286

Chapter 3
Art.IWM ART 2957; Documents.9506/A; Q 5794; Q35825d; Q 67249; Q 795; Q 98; Q 113; Art.IWM ART 2385; Q 23;

Chapter 4
Q 753; Q 744; Q 796; Q 754; Documents.11213/B © S Bond; Documents.11213/O; Q 52; Q 745; Q 4307; FIR 9151; Art.IWM ART 4463; Q 755; Q 739; HU 112461; HU 112462; Q 772; Q 746; EPH 5239; Documents.12701

In Focus: The Film of the Battle
Q 11846; IWM FLM 1673; Q 79501; Q 70166; Q 70164; Q 79503; Q 79478; Art. IWM PST 7227

Chapter 5
Q 800; Q 775; Q 758; Q 872; Q 4002; Q 4150; Documents. 8175; Q 1259; Q 4056; Q 49076; Documents.14531; Q 824; UNI 10830; Q 3990; Q 61359; Documents.20535 © V Cockcroft; Q 183; Q 991; Documents.10798 © Julia S Rush; WEA 3092; Art.IWM PST 12968; Art. IWM PST 6317; Q 23746

In Focus: British War Photography and the Somme
Q 24087; Q 45365; Q 29; Q 55; Q 716; HU 108196; Q 4203; Q 67719; Q 2486;

Chapter 6
CO 802; CO 202; Q 5572; Documents.21817; Art.IWM ART 2121; CO 766; Q 5578; Q 194; Q 4271; Q 11617; OMD 5445-5451

Chapter 7
Art.IWM ART 3006; Art.IWM ART 2377; FEQ 314; Q 27637; Q 27639; Art.IWM ART 2098; FIR 11492; WEA 835.1; UNI 288; Q 1439; FEQ 25; INS 7583; FLA 967; Q 2980; Q 4602; Q 4510; Q 1582; Q 4593

In Focus: Art and the Somme
Art.IWM ART 5911 © The Shepard Trust; Art.IWM ART 4476; Q 854; Art. IWM ART 4471; Art.IWM ART 2049; Art.IWM ART 2161; Art.IWM ART 2993; Art.IWM ART 2955; Art.IWM ART 1145; Art.IWM ART 520; Art.IWM ART 1887

Chapter 8
E(AUS) 166; HU 58985; Q 2041; Art.IWM ART 2995; Q 65442; Q 905; Art.IWM ART 5501; Q 1526; Art.IWM ART 2997; Q 1828; Q 4586; Q 57515; IWM_2006_20-005

CREDITS

Interview with William Underwood (IWM Sound 4247), BBC copyright material reproduced courtesy of the British Broadcasting Corporation. All rights reserved.

Private papers of William Lafrichoud (Documents.17626), © The Estate of W Lafrichoud

Private papers of Rowland Luther (Documents.1325), © The Estate of R M Luther

Interview with Horace Astin (IWM Sound 11039), © Mrs Gladys Harrison

Private papers of Thomas Jennings (Documents.6596), © The Estate of T A Jennings

Private papers of Harold Yeo (Documents.3132), © The Estate of Colonel H E Yeo

Private papers of Bernard Stevenson (Documents.4481), © The Estate of W B Stevenson

Private papers of Harry Bursey (Documents.5646), © Miss Victoria Thomas

Private papers of Harold Wyllie (Documents.3862), © The Estate of Lieutenant Colonel H Wyllie

Private papers of R H V Buxton (Documents.20428), © The Estate of Captain R H V Buxton

Private papers of Hubert Rees (Documents.7166), © Diana Stockford

Private papers of William Colyer (Documents.7256), © The Estate of Captain W T Colyer

Private papers of Alfred Bundy (Documents.10828), © The Estate of Major A E Bundy

The Spectator, 25 August 1916, p.3

Private papers of Cyril José (Documents.19925), © Ron Alpe

Private papers of Geoffrey Lillywhite (Documents.7226), © The Estate of Colonel G Lillywhite

Private papers of Harold Horne (Documents.4867), © The Estate of Captain H Horne

Interview with Stuart Hastie (IWM Sound 4126), BBC copyright material reproduced courtesy of the British Broadcasting Corporation. All rights reserved.

Interview with Marjorie Llewelyn (IWM Sound 4163), BBC copyright material reproduced courtesy of the British Broadcasting Corporation. All rights reserved.

Our BC Post, Copse B, near Maricourt, Somme, August 1916 by E H Shepard (Art.IWM ART 5911), reproduced with permission of Curtis Brown Group Ltd, London on behalf of The Shepard Trust, copyright © The Shepard Trust

ACKNOWLEDGEMENTS

Although my name is on the cover, this book has been a collaborative effort and it is only fair that I acknowledge the important contribution made by a number of my IWM colleagues. Ellen Parton, Roger Smither, Alan Wakefield and Richard Slocombe all provided vital assistance in terms of both expertly written text and advice on illustrations, while Madeleine James was the mastermind who co-ordinated such a large and at times complicated publishing project, ably assisted by Caitlin Flynn.

Thanks should also go to Nigel Steel and Laurie Milner, who developed IWM's 2006 web exhibition on the Battle of the Somme which inspired this book. Miranda Harrison, who did an excellent job of copy-editing, Stephen Long, our fantastic designer, and Kay Heather, who handled the production, also deserve my thanks. Historical narratives of this kind are only as strong as the original sources upon which they are based, and I should therefore like to particularly thank the families and copyright holders who gave permission for the many personal accounts to be included.

ANTHONY RICHARDS

Anthony is the Head of IWM's Documents and Sound Section. For many years he has worked on the diaries, letters and memoirs in the museum's care and is responsible for its extensive collection of personal stories in both written and recorded form. A qualified archivist, Anthony has also written *In Their Own Words: Untold Stories from the First World War* (published by IWM in 2016).

INDEX